Rachel De-lahay

The Westbridge

T0262481

B L O O M S B U R Y

LONDON • NEW DELHI • NEW YORK • SYDNEY

Bloomsbury Methuen Drama
An imprint of Bloomsbury Publishing Plc

50 Bedford Square   1385 Broadway
London   New York
WC1B 3DP   NY 10018
UK   USA

www.bloomsbury.com

Bloomsbury is a registered trade mark of Bloomsbury Publishing Plc

First published 2011
Reprinted 2013

British Library Cataloguing-in-Publication Data
A catalogue record for this book is available from the British Library.

ISBN: PB: 978-1-4081-7201-8
      EPDF: 978-1-4081-7200-1
      EPUB: 978-1-4081-7199-8

Library of Congress Cataloging-in-Publication Data
A catalog record for this book is available from the Library of Congress.

Typeset by Mark Heslington Ltd, Scarborough, North Yorkshire

ROYAL COURT

The Royal Court Theatre presents

THE WESTBRIDGE

by **Rachel De-lahay**

THE WESTBRIDGE was first performed at the The Bussey Building, Peckham Rye on Thursday 3rd November 2011 as part of the Theatre Local Season.

THE WESTBRIDGE was first performed at the Royal Court Jerwood Theatre Upstairs, Sloane Square, London on Friday 25th November 2011.

THE WESTBRIDGE was developed with the support of the Paul Hamlyn Foundation as part of Unheard Voices: A Paul Hamlyn Foundation Project and produced as part of Jerwood New Playwrights, supported by the Jerwood Charitable Foundation.

Theatre Local is sponsored by

Bloomberg

Principal Sponsor

THE WESTBRIDGE

by Rachel De-lahay

Andre **Ryan Calais Cameron**

Audrey **Jo Martin**

Soriya **Chetna Pandya**

Marcus **Fraser Ayres**

Georgina **Daisy Lewis**

Saghir **Paul Bhattacharjee**

Ibi **Ray Panthaki**

Old Lady **Adlyn Ross**

Sara **Shavani Seth**

Boy **Samuel Foray**

Director **Clint Dyer**

Designer **Ultz**

Lighting Designer **Katharine Williams**

Sound Designer **Emma Laxton**

Casting Director **Amy Ball**

Assistant Director **Kuldip Powar**

Assistant Designers **Sadeysa Greenaway-Bailey, Mark Simmonds**

Production Manager **Tariq Rifaat**

Stage Managers **Julia Slienger, Alison Rich**

Stage Management Work Pacement **Shannon Joyce Foster**

Fight Director **Alison De Burgh**

Costume Supervisor **Iona Kenrick, Amita Kilumanga**

Scenic Painter **Jodie Pritchard**

The Royal Court and Stage Management wish to thank the following for their help with this production: AJW Props, Annie at Aldershot Household Waste & Recycling Centre, Asda, Almeida Theatre, Breakaway Effects Ltd, Neil Cooper at Brackenwood, Donmar Warehouse, Hampstead Theatre, Steve Murray at Furniture at Work, Marks & Spencers, Mickey Smith and staff of the CLF at The Bussey Building, Vanessa Stone, Tash Shepherd, Tesco, Tricycle Theatre, Waitrose, Yvonne Arnaud Theatre.

Rachel De-lahay is the recipient of the inaugural Clare McIntyre Bursary, a financial award given to an emerging playwright in memory of the playwright Clare McIntyre.

THE COMPANY

RACHEL DE-LAHAY (Writer)

The Westbridge, formally SW11, was born out of the Royal Court Unheard Voices writers' group. It won the 2010 Alfred Fagon award and is Rachel's first play. Rachel also works as an actress and is currently working on a new play having been selected as one of the BBC Writersroom 10, with the Bush as her partner theatre.

FRASER AYRES (Marcus)

FOR THE ROYAL COURT: Rampage, Workers Writes, Four and Bluebird.

OTHER THEATRE INCLUDES: What Would Judas Do? (GreyScale); Mercury Fur (Paines Plough); The People Next Door (Traverse, Edinburgh/Stratford East); Ramayana (National); Vurt (Contact); Telling Tales (Lyric Hammersmith); The Loves of Lady Purple (Mouse People); Sandman (National/Leicester, Haymarket).

TELEVISION INCLUDES: Casualty, Grown Ups, W10 LDN, Little Ms Jocelyn, The Omid Djalili Show, The Burglar Diaries/Thieves Like Us, Vital Signs, Wide Sargasso Sea, The Smoking Room, Bella and The Boys, Frances Tuesday, Dogma TV – Fierce, Merseybeat, Trail of Guilt, Swivel on the Tip, The Vice, Urban Gothic, London's Burning.

FILM INCLUDES: Heartless, Adulthood, Intimacy, It Was An Accident, Rage, Speak Like A Child, The Opportunist, Just One Kiss, Dinner for Two.

AWARDS INCLUDE: 2004 Herald Angel Best Actor of Edinburgh Fringe Festival for The People Next Door, 2005 Time Out Award Best Actor for The People Next Door.

PAUL BHATTACHARJEE (Saghir)

FOR THE ROYAL COURT: Disconnect, Blood, Iranian Nights, Lalita's Way, Mohair, The Burrow.

OTHER THEATRE INCLUDES: On The Record (Arcola); Faith, Hope & Charity (Southwark Playhouse); Arabian Nights, Edward III, The Island Princess, The Malcontent, The Roman Actor (RSC); The Great Game, Guantanamo, Fashion (Tricycle); A Disappearing Number (Complicite - Barbican/World Tour); Playing with Fire, Murmuring Judges (National); Blood Wedding (Almeida); Twelfth Night (Albery); The Mayor of Zalamea (Liverpool Everyman); Hobson's Choice (Young Vic); Arabian Nights (Young Vic/World Tour); Seagull, Present Laughter, The Tempest, A Perfect Ganesh (West Yorkshire Playhouse); Indian Ink (Aldwych); Yes, Memsahib, Inkalaab 1919, Vilayat, England, Your England, Sacrifice, The Lion's Raj, Ancestral Voices, Meet Me, Chilli In Your Eyes, The Little Clay Cart, The Broken Thigh, Abduction Of Draupadi, Exile in The Forest, Bicharo, Sweet Dreams (Tara Arts 1979-97).

TELEVISION INCLUDES: The Jury, Any Human Heart, Eastenders, Britz, Waking the Dead, New Tricks, Spooks, The Bill, Bedtime, Rosemary & Thyme, The Jury, Hawk, Navy in Action, Thieftakers, Wing and a Prayer, Turning World, Two Oranges and a Mango, Inkalaab, Ancestral Voices, Chilli in Your Eyes, Johnny Jarvis, Pravina's Wedding, Maigret, Albion Market, Lovebirds, Shalom, Salaam, Bergerac, Here is the News, Saracen, Northern Crescent, Black and Blue, Clubland, Sister Wife, A Summer Day's Dream.

FILM INCLUDES: Casino Royale, The Best Exotic Marigold Hotel, White Teeth, Dirty Pretty Things, Jinnah, Wild West.

RADIO INCLUDES: Silver Street (regular).

RYAN CALAIS CAMERON (Andre)

THEATRE INCLUDES: Coyote Was Going There (Light House Theatre).

FILM & TELEVISION INCLUDES: Better Dayz, Blame the Parents, Fractured, Tree of Light, Yesterday's Tomorrow, A Week in January, The Corridor, Mad Frank, NO ID, People's Execution, Turning Point, Vengeance of a Dead Man, Over Stanley.

CLINT DYER (Director)

FOR THE ROYAL COURT: Emergency (also writer).

OTHER THEATRE INCLUDES: The Big Life (Theatre Royal Stratford East/West End).

FILM INCLUDES: Pukka, One of Us, Second Chance.

Clint has acted extensively in theatre such as SUS (Young Vic), Big White Fog (Almeida) and films such as SUS, Unknown, The Trail, Agora, Cherps, Mr Inbetween, Sahara.

SAMUEL FOLAY (Boy)

THEATRE INCLUDES: A Midsummer Night's Madness (Hackney Empire/Edinburgh Festival); Team Spirit (Tricycle).

FILM INCLUDES: The Man Inside, Tooting Broadway, The Affected.

EMMA LAXTON (Sound Designer)

FOR THE ROYAL COURT: The Heretic, Off the Endz, Tusk Tusk, Faces in the Crowd, That Face (& Duke of York's), Gone Too Far!, Catch, Scenes From The Back Of Beyond, Woman and Scarecrow, The World's Biggest Diamond, Incomplete & Random Acts of Kindness, My Name is Rachel Corrie (& Playhouse/Minetta Lane, New York/Galway Festival/Edinburgh Festival), Bone, The Weather, Bear Hug, Terrorism, Food Chain.

OTHER THEATRE INCLUDES: If There Is I Haven't Found It Yet, 2nd May 1997, Apologia, The Contingency Plan, Wrecks, Broken Space Season, 2000 Feet Away, Tinderbox (Bush); Timing (King's Head), Ghosts (ATC at Arcola), Treasure Island (Theatre Royal Haymarket); A Chistmas Carol (Chichester Festival Theatre); Welcome to Ramallah (iceandfire); Pornography (Birmingham Rep/Traverse); Shoot/Get Treasure/Repeat (National); Europe (Dundee Rep/Barbican Pit); Other Hands (Soho); The Unthinkable (Sheffield Crucible); My Dad's a Birdman (Young Vic); The Gods Are Not To Blame (Arcola); Late Fragment (Tristan Bates).

DAISY LEWIS (Georgina)

FOR THE ROYAL COURT: Seven Jewish Children, The Good Family.

OTHER THEATRE INCLUDES: Amazonia (Young Vic); Three Sisters on Hope Street (Hampstead/Liverpool Everyman); Silence, Blue Moon Over Poplar (NYT); Antigone at Hell's Mouth (NYT/Kneehigh); The Good Person of Szechuan (Chelsea Theatre).

TELEVISION INCLUDES: Lewis, Miss Austen Regrets, After You've Gone, Doctor Who.

FILM INCLUDES: Pusher, Lotus Eaters, From Time to Time.

JO MARTIN (Audrey)

FOR THE ROYAL COURT: Majic.

OTHER THEATRE INCLUDES: Everything Must Go (Soho); The Frontline (Shakespeare's Globe); Family Man, Ready or Not, Funny Black Women on the Edge, Eldorado (Stratford East); Noughts and Crosses, Oroonoko, Don Carlos (RSC); Coyote on a Fence (Royal Exhange, Manchester/Duchess Theatre, West End); Somewhere the Shadow, Meridian (Contact, Manchester); Victor and the Ladies, Pecong (Tricycle); Job Rocking (Riverside Studios); To Kill a Mockingbird (Mermaid Theatre); A Temporary Rupture (Cockpit/Croydon Warehouse/tour); Beef No Chicken, Dog (Shaw Theatre); Nobody's Back Yard (Umoja).

TELEVISION INCLUDES: George and Bernard Shaw, The Culshaw and Stephenson Show, Holby City, Katy Brand's Big Ass Show, Stupid, Doctors, All About George, Tunnel of Love, Kerching, The Bill, The Crouch's, 40 Acres and a Mule, Casualty, A&E, Supergirlie, The Murder of Stephen Lawrence, Blouse and Skirt, The Real McCoy, Chef, Birds of a Feather, Dodgems, The Brittas Empire, Club Mix.

FILM INCLUDES: Chalet Girl, 4321, Batman Begins, Dead Meat, I Love My Mum, For Queen and Country, The Godsend, Cheeky.

RADIO INCLUDES: Vent, Silver Street, School Plays, Little Big Women, Windrush, Emerald Green.

AWARDS INCLUDE: 2001 BFM International Film Festival Best Actress Award for Dead Meat.

CHETNA PANDYA (Soriya)

FOR THE ROYAL COURT: Shades, The Spiral (Rough Cut).

OTHER THEATRE INCLUDES: Arabian Nights (RSC); Hens! (Riverside Studios); Behud (Soho/Belgrade, Coventry); A Disappearing Number (Complicite/Barbican/Novello, West End/World Tour); Deadeye (Birmingham Rep/Soho); Coram Boy (National); Lucky Stiff (New Wimbledon Studio); Romeo & Juliet (Changeling Theatre Company).

FILM & TELEVISION INCLUDES: RA1, Black Mirror – The National Anthem, Casualty, Hens!, Identity, Holby Blue, Broken News, The Worst Week of My Life, Green Wing, The Message, New Tricks, Doctors.

RADIO INCLUDES: A Disappearing Number, Bora Bistra.

RAY PANTHAKI (Ibi)

FOR THE ROYAL COURT: Where Do We Live?, I Come From There: New Plays from the Arab World.

OTHER THEATRE INCLUDES: In My Name (Old Red Lion/Trafalgar Studios); Gladiator Games (Sheffield Theatre/Stratford East).

TELEVISION INCLUDES: Mongrels, Strictly Confidential, Blessed, Bad Press, Eastenders (regular), Doctors, Spooks, My Family, Blood Strangers, The Armando Ianucci Show, Losing It, The Bill.

FILM INCLUDES: Kidulthood, 28 Days Later, Ali G Indahouse, Rehab, It's A Wonderful Afterlife, City Rats, The Feral Generation, Bollywood Queen, Tube Tales, Screwed, The Man Inside, Interview with a Hitman.

RADIO INCLUDES: Rudolfo's Zest.

KULDIP POWAR (Assistant Director)

THEATRE: (Assiociate Artist-Tamasha) Mentoring writers on Small Lives Global Ties (Tamasha Scratch Night-Unicorn Theatre).

FILM (As Director): Kabhi Ritz Kabhie Palladiuim, Remembrance, For The Record – The Social Life Of Indian Vinyl in Southall, Unravelling, Presence, Hope.

SHAVANI SETH (Sara)

THEATRE INCLUDES: The Unfortunate Love of the British Empire (Hackney Empire/Theatre Space); There is Nothing There (Oval House); FML (ICA).

FILM & TELEVISION INCLUDES: Life in My Shoes, Casualty, Documental, Tooting Broadway.

ADLYN ROSS (Old lady)

THEATRE INCLUDES: Meri Christmas (tour); Bombay Dreams (West End); My Dad's Corner Shop (Birmingham Rep); Balti Kings (West Yorkshire Playhouse); Emeralds and Diamonds (Parallel Existence); Twelfth Night (British Council tour); Bravely Fought The Queen (Border Crossings); Dream for a Hero (Lyric Hammersmith).

TELEVISION INCLUDES: Little Crackers, Doctors, Coronation Street, The Playground, Holby City, Casualty, Bob Martin, Heartburn Hotel, Flight, My Sister Wife, Intercity Welcome, Kinsey, The Children's Act.

FILM INCLUDES: Lost Christmas, It's A Wonderful Afterlife, Bend It Like Beckham, The Great Trilby, Bhaji on the Beach.

ULTZ (Designer)

FOR THE ROYAL COURT: 40 years ago ULTZ's first professional job was here, as Assistant Designer on the World Premiere of Edward Bond's Lear. More recently he designed Jerusalem (& West End/ Broadway), Chicken Soup with Barley, Off The Endz, Wig Out!, The Family Plays, The Winterling, Stoning Mary, A Girl in a Car with a Man, Fresh Kills, The Weather, Bone, Fallout, The Night Heron, Fireface, Lift Off, Mojo (& Steppenwolf, Chicago).

OTHER RECENT THEATRE INCLUDES: designs for The Beauty Queen Of Leenane (Young Vic/Dublin Gaiety/UK Tour); Annie Get Your Gun, Hobson's Choice, A Respectable Wedding (Young Vic); Blue/Orange, Iya-Ile, The Estate, The Gods Are Not To Blame (Tiata Fahodzi at Arcola/Soho Theatre); Blood & Gifts, The Ramayana (National).

RECENT OPERA INCLUDES: designing the set for Il Tabarro (Royal Opera House); sets and costumes for The Bitter Tears of Petra Von Kant (& Theater Basel); Cavalleria Rusticana/I Pagliacci (ENO); Macbeth, Falstaff (Glyndebourne); Lohengrin (Bavarian State Opera); directing & designing Idomeneo, White Horse Inn, Hansel und Gretel, Salome, Der Rosengarten, Die Fledermaus (Landestheater-Niederbayern, Germany).

AS AN ASSOCIATE ARTIST AT THEATRE ROYAL STRATFORD EAST: develops and directs new pieces of Urban Music Theatre – Pied Piper (& Barbican/UK Tour); The Blacks Remixed (co-directed), Da Boyz; designed The Harder They Come (& Barbican/UK Tour/Toronto/ Miami).

RECENT AWARDS: Best Set Design, Olivier Award 2010 for Jerusalem; Best Set Design, Off West End Awards 2011 for The Beauty Queen of Leenane; Outstanding achievement in an Affiliate Theatre, Olivier Award 2007 for Pied Piper – A Hip Hop Dance Revolution.

KATHARINE WILLIAMS (Lighting Designer)

Katharine works primarily in drama, dance and physical theatre, with some opera, musical and circus projects, and creates dynamic, strong, image-driven work. Her designs have been seen in China, Hong Kong, New Zealand, Canada, USA, Mexico, Ireland, Holland, Spain, Italy, Germany, Luxembourg, Armenia, Romania, Russia and the Czech Republic

THEATRE INCLUDES: Invisible (Transport Theatre); The Tempest (Jericho House/Barbican); The Pajama Men (Assembly Theatre); Bette and Joan: The Final Curtain (Foursight Theatre); Closer (Théâtre Des Capucins); Faeries (Royal Opera House); Landscape & Monologue (Theatre Royal Bath); Ivan and the Dogs (Atc/Soho Theatre); Joined Up Thinking (Young Vic); The Goat, Or Who Is Sylvia? (Traverse Theatre), Reykjavic (Shams); Nocturnal (The Gate); Amgen: Broken (Sherman Cymru/Theatr Clywd); Dolls (National Theatre Scotland); I Am Falling (Gate Theatre/Sadler's Wells); Touched…For The Very First Time (Trafalgar Studios).

JERWOOD CHARITABLE FOUNDATION

Since 1994 Jerwood New Playwrights has supported the production of 70 new plays by emerging playwrights at the Royal Court including Joe Penhall's SOME VOICES, Mark Ravenhill's SHOPPING AND FUCKING (co-production with Out of Joint), Ayub Khan Din's EAST IS EAST (co-production with Tamasha), Martin McDonagh's THE BEAUTY QUEEN OF LEENANE (co-production with Druid Theatre Company), Conor McPherson's THE WEIR, Nick Grosso's REAL CLASSY AFFAIR, Sarah Kane's 4.48 PSYCHOSIS, Gary Mitchell's THE FORCE OF CHANGE, David Eldridge's UNDER THE BLUE SKY, David Harrower's PRESENCE, Simon Stephens' HERONS, Roy Williams' CLUBLAND, Leo Butler's REDUNDANT, Michael Wynne's THE PEOPLE ARE FRIENDLY, David Greig's OUTLYING ISLANDS, Zinnie Harris' NIGHTINGALE AND CHASE, Grae Cleugh's FUCKING GAMES, Rona Munro's IRON, Richard Bean's UNDER THE WHALEBACK, Ché Walker's FLESH WOUND, Roy Williams' FALLOUT, Mick Mahoney's FOOD CHAIN, Ayub Khan Din's NOTES ON FALLING LEAVES, Leo Butler's LUCKY DOG, Simon Stephens' COUNTRY MUSIC, Laura Wade's BREATHING CORPSES, Debbie Tucker Green's STONING MARY, David Eldridge's INCOMPLETE AND RANDOM ACTS OF KINDNESS, Gregory Burke's ON TOUR, Stella Feehily's O GO MY MAN, Simon Stephens' MOTORTOWN, Simon Farquhar's RAINBOW KISS, April de Angelis, Stella Feehily, Tanika Gupta, Chloe Moss and Laura Wade's CATCH, Mike Bartlett's MY CHILD, Polly Stenham's THAT FACE, Alexi Kaye Campbell's THE PRIDE, Fiona Evans' SCARBOROUGH, Levi David Addai's OXFORD STREET, Bola Agbaje's GONE TOO FAR!, Alia Bano's SHADES, Polly Stenham's TUSK TUSK, Tim Crouch's THE AUTHOR, Bola Agbaje's OFF THE ENDZ, DC Moore's THE EMPIRE and Anya Reiss' SPUR OF THE MOMENT.

So far in 2011 Jerwood New Playwrights has supported Anya Reiss' THE ACID TEST and Penelope Skinner's THE VILLAGE BIKE. Jerwood New Playwrights is supported by the Jerwood Charitable Foundation.

The Jerwood Charitable Foundation is dedicated to imaginative and responsible revenue funding of the arts, supporting artists to develop and grow at important stages in their careers. They work with artists across art forms, from dance and theatre to literature, music and the visual arts. www.jerwoodcharitablefoundation.org.

Anya Reiss' THE ACID TEST
(photo: Manuel Harlan)

Penelope Skinner's THE VILLAGE BIKE
(photo: Keith Pattison)

THE ENGLISH STAGE COMPANY
AT THE ROYAL COURT THEATRE

'For me the theatre is really a religion or way of life.
You must decide what you feel the world is about
and what you want to say about it, so that everything
in the theatre you work in is saying the same thing
... A theatre must have a recognisable attitude. It will
have one, whether you like it or not.'

George Devine, first artistic director of the
English Stage Company: notes for an unwritten
book.

photo: Stephen Cummiskey

As Britain's leading national company dedicated to new work, the Royal Court Theatre produces
new plays of the highest quality, working with writers from all backgrounds, and addressing the
problems and possibilities of our time.

"The Royal Court has been at the centre of British cultural life for the past 50 years, an engine
room for new writing and constantly transforming the theatrical culture." Stephen Daldry

Since its foundation in 1956, the Royal Court has presented premieres by almost every leading
contemporary British playwright, from John Osborne's Look Back in Anger to Caryl Churchill's
A Number and Tom Stoppard's Rock 'n' Roll. Just some of the other writers to have chosen the
Royal Court to premiere their work include Edward Albee, John Arden, Richard Bean, Samuel
Beckett, Edward Bond, Leo Butler, Jez Butterworth, Martin Crimp, Ariel Dorfman, Stella Feehily,
Christopher Hampton, David Hare, Eugène Ionesco, Ann Jellicoe, Terry Johnson, Sarah Kane, David
Mamet, Martin McDonagh, Conor McPherson, Joe Penhall, Lucy Prebble, Mark Ravenhill, Simon
Stephens, Wole Soyinka, Polly Stenham, David Storey, Debbie Tucker Green, Arnold Wesker and
Roy Williams.

"It is risky to miss a production there." Financial Times

In addition to its full-scale productions, the Royal Court also facilitates international work at a
grass roots level, developing exchanges which bring young writers to Britain and sending British
writers, actors and directors to work with artists around the world. The research and play
development arm of the Royal Court Theatre, The Studio, finds the most exciting and diverse
range of new voices in the UK. The Studio runs play-writing groups including the Young Writers
Programme, Critical Mass for black, Asian and minority ethnic writers and the biennial Young
Writers Festival. For further information, go to www.royalcourttheatre.com/playwriting/the-
studio.

"Yes, the Royal Court is on a roll. Yes, Dominic Cooke has just the genius and kick that this venue
needs... It's fist-bitingly exciting." Independent

ROYAL COURT SUPPORTERS

The Royal Court is able to offer its unique playwriting and audience development programmes because of significant and longstanding partnerships with the organisations that support it.

Coutts is the Principal Sponsor of the Royal Court. The Genesis Foundation supports the Royal Court's work with International Playwrights. Theatre Local is sponsored by Bloomberg. The Jerwood Charitable Foundation supports new plays by playwrights through the Jerwood New Playwrights series. The Artistic Director's Chair is supported by a lead grant from The Peter Jay Sharp Foundation, contributing to the activities of the Artistic Director's office. Over the past ten years the BBC has supported the Gerald Chapman Fund for directors.

The Harold Pinter Playwright's Award is given annually by his widow, Lady Antonia Fraser, to support a new commission at the Royal Court.

PUBLIC FUNDING
Arts Council England, London
British Council
European Commission Representation in the UK

CHARITABLE DONATIONS
American Friends of the Royal Court
Martin Bowley Charitable Trust
The Brim Foundation*
Gerald Chapman Fund
City Bridge Trust
Cowley Charitable Trust
The H and G de Freitas Charitable Trust
The Dorset Foundation
The John Ellerman Foundation
The Eranda Foundation
Genesis Foundation
J Paul Getty Jnr Charitable Trust
The Golden Bottle Trust
The Haberdashers' Company
Paul Hamlyn Foundation
Jerwood Charitable Foundation
Marina Kleinwort Charitable Trust
The Leathersellers' Company
John Lyon's Charity
The Andrew W Mellon Foundation
The Laura Pels Foundation*
Jerome Robbins Foundation*
Rose Foundation
Royal Victoria Hall Foundation
The Dr Mortimer & Theresa Sackler Foundation
The Peter Jay Sharp Foundation*
The Steel Charitable Trust
John Thaw Foundation
The Garfield Weston Foundation

CORPORATE SUPPORTERS & SPONSORS
BBC
Bloomberg
Coutts
Ecosse Films
Grey London
Kudos Film & Television
MAC
Moët & Chandon
Oakley Capital Limited
Sky Arts
Smythson of Bond Street
White Light Ltd

BUSINESS ASSOCIATES, MEMBERS & BENEFACTORS
Auerbach & Steele Opticians
Bank of America Merrill Lynch
Hugo Boss
Lazard
Louis Vuitton
Oberon Books
Peter Jones
Savills
Vanity Fair

DEVELOPMENT ADVOCATES
John Ayton
Elizabeth Bandeen
Kinvara Balfour
Anthony Burton
Piers Butler
Sindy Caplan
Sarah Chappatte
Cas Donald (Vice Chair)
Allie Esiri
Celeste Fenichel
Emma Marsh (Chair)
William Russell
Deborah Shaw Marquardt (Vice Chair)
Sian Westerman
Nick Wheeler
Daniel Winterfeldt

Supported by
ARTS COUNCIL ENGLAND

FOR THE ROYAL COURT

Royal Court Theatre, Sloane Square, London SW1W 8AS
Tel: 020 7565 5050 Fax: 020 7565 5001
info@royalcourttheatre.com, www.royalcourttheatre.com

Artistic Director **Dominic Cooke**
Associate Directors **Simon Godwin, Jeremy Herrin*, Sacha Wares***
Artistic Associate **Emily McLaughlin***
Diversity Associate **Ola Animashawun***
Education Associate **Lynne Gagliano***
PA to the Artistic Director **Pamela Wilson**

Literary Manager **Christopher Campbell**
Senior Reader **Nicola Wass****
Literary Assistant **Marcelo Dos Santos**
Studio Administrator **Clare McQuillan**
Studio Assistant **Tom Lyons***
Writers' Tutor **Leo Butler***
Pearson Playwright **DC Moore ^**

Associate Director International **Elyse Dodgson**
International Projects Manager **Chris James**

Casting Director **Amy Ball**
Casting Assistant **Lotte Hines**

Head of Production **Paul Handley**
JTU Production Manager **Tariq Rifaat**
Production Assistant **Zoe Hurwitz**
Head of Lighting **Matt Drury**
Lighting Deputy **Stephen Andrews**
Lighting Assistants **Katie Pitt, Jack Williams**
Lighting Board Operator **Jack Champion**
Head of Stage **Steven Stickler**
Stage Deputy **Dan Lockett**
Stage Chargehand **Lee Crimmen**
Chargehand Carpenter **Richard Martin**
Head of Sound **David McSeveney**
Sound Deputy **Alex Caplen**
Sound Operator **Sam Charleston**
Head of Costume **Iona Kenrick**
Costume Deputy **Jackie Orton**
Wardrobe Assistant **Pam Anson**

Executive Director **Kate Horton**
General Manager **Catherine Thornborrow**
Administrative Assistant **Holly Handel**

Head of Finance & Administration **Helen Perryer**
Senior Finance & Administration Officer
Martin Wheeler
Finance Officer **Rachel Harrison***
Finance & Administration Assistant **Tessa Rivers**
Finance & Administration Assistant (Maternity Cover)
Rosie Mortimer

Head of Marketing & Sales **Becky Wootton**
Acting Marketing Manager **Helen Slater**
Press & Public Relations Officer **Anna Evans**
Communications Officer **Ruth Hawkins**
Communications Interns **Charlie Metcalf, Leila Sellers**

Sales Manager **Kevin West**
Deputy Sales Manager **Liam Geoghegan**
Box Office Sales Assistants **Joe Hodgson, Carla Kingham*, Stephen Laughton*, Helen Murray*, Ciara O'Toole, Helen Preddy**

Head of Development **Gaby Styles**
Senior Development Manager **Hannah Clifford**
Development Managers **Lucy Buxton, Luciana Lawlor**
Development Officer **Penny Saward**
Development Intern **Dean Stigwood**

Theatre Manager **Bobbie Stokes**
Front of House Manager **Rachel Dudley**
Events Manager **Joanna Ostrom**
Duty Managers **Fiona Clift*, Elinor Keber***
Front of House Assistant **Deirdre Lennon***
Bar & Food Manager **Sami Rifaat**
Deputy Bar & Food Manager **Ali Christian**
Interim Head Chef **Tim Jenner**
Sous Chef **Paulino Chuitcheu**
Bookshop Manager **Simon David**
Bookshop Assistants **Vanessa Hammick***
Stage Door/Reception **Paul Lovegrove, Tyrone Lucas**

Thanks to all of our ushers and bar staff.

^This theatre has the support of the Pearson Playwrights' Scheme sponsored by the Peggy Ramsay Foundation.

** The post of Senior Reader is supported by NoraLee & Jon Sedmak through the American Friends of the Royal Court Theatre.

* Part-time.

ENGLISH STAGE COMPANY

President
Dame Joan Plowright CBE

Honorary Council
Sir Richard Eyre CBE
Alan Grieve CBE
Martin Paisner CBE

Council
Chairman **Anthony Burton**
Vice Chairman **Graham Devlin CBE**

Members
Jennette Arnold OBE
Judy Daish
Sir David Green KCMG
Joyce Hytner OBE
Stephen Jeffreys
Wasfi Kani OBE
Phyllida Lloyd CBE
James Midgley
Sophie Okonedo OBE
Alan Rickman
Anita Scott
Katharine Viner
Stewart Wood

The Westbridge

Characters
(in order of appearance)

Andre – *sixteen years old, Black British*
Audrey – *Andre's mom, Jamaican*
Soriya – *in her twenties, mixed race White-Pakistani*
Marcus – *in his twenties, mixed race White-Afro-Caribbean*
George – *in her twenties, White British*
Ibi – *Soriya's brother, late twenties*
Saghir – *Soriya's dad, Pakistani*
Old Lady – *Pakistani*
Sara – *sixteen years old, British Asian*

The play is set in Battersea, south west London.

Act One

Scene One

Andre *walks into his house. Night. Light gets flicked on and we see* **Audrey** *sat at the table.* **Andre**'s *shocked to see her.*

Andre   Rare! Soz I'm late.

Audrey   And you think that's the magic password that will get you upstairs?

Andre   I said I'm sorry.

Beat.

Audrey   Carry on, yeah? You just carry on.

Andre *kisses his teeth.*

Andre   Yeah yeah.

Andre *walks past her.*

Audrey   You know what? Get out!

Andre   What?

Audrey   You hard a hearing? I've had enough.

Andre   And where do you expect me to go?

Audrey   Now, how's about to one of your croneys' houses?!

Andre   What are you on about 'croney'?!

Audrey   – or wherever the fuck it is you are when you're not in here night after night!

Andre   You know where I am! I was at Tyrone's house!

Audrey   You think I'm stupid? You think I never call Tyrone's house?

Andre   No one don't answer the phone over there –

Audrey   Same way you don't answer your mobile?!

Andre   It was on silent!

Audrey   And when you seen the missed calls?

Andre   I never had any credit.

Beat.

Audrey   I moved us from that estate to give you a chance, ya hear? And every night you have me walk back up there looking for you.

Andre   You walked up to Westbridge?

Audrey   Oh, yes.

Andre   And?

Audrey   Ya blind? Ya nah see what a gwarn up there?

Andre   Not really, I was at Tyrone's.

Audrey   Funny that. When my man locking up shop, tells me how a bag of mans were in there not long earlier. One on bike, fitting your description.

Andre   So? We went shop.

Audrey   You and five boys Shirley let sit up in her house 'til all hours?

Andre   No. I was at Tyrone's and we bumped into the rest of the mans outside the shop, innit?

Audrey   I swear to Jesus! You tell me you were at Tyrone's one more time, I will kick your head through that bloodclart wall!

Andre   Differently! I was at Tyrone's! Fucking phone him! 'Bout you wanna kick mans' heads in! Go on then! Dare ya! Feh!

Audrey   Oh, so you're a bad man now? Now you've been walking 'pon street all night?

Andre   Walking stre— I'm not gonna tell you again! I was at Tyrone's!

Andre *turns to exit when we hear a banging on the front door.*

Audrey   Get upstairs!

Andre   Who the fuck's that?

Audrey   I said get upstairs!

Banging again. **Andre** *stays.*

Asian Man   Open the fucking door you piece of shit!

Audrey   Move from me door 'fore I call the police!

Asian Man   You think I haven't called them already? That fucking piece of . . . ! Open up!

Audrey *quickly reaches for her mobile phone.*

Audrey   Andre get upstairs!

Asian Man   Oi! Open now or I kick down bloody fucking door!

Audrey (*on phone*)   Police.

Andre *picks up a heavy ornament off the table and stands near the door ready. We hear the sound of sirens outside. The man kicks the door out of frustration.*

Asian Man   I will fucking kill you!

We hear a softer knock on the door.

Voice   Hello? Open up! It's the police!

Andre   Mom?

Audrey *hangs up her mobile, looks at* **Andre** *who lowers his arm with the ornament.*

Audrey (*to* **Andre**)   You were at Tyrone's all night.

Andre   I was!

Beat.

Audrey   Coming!

Audrey *goes to open the door.*

Lights.

Scene Two

George *and* **Soriya**'s *kitchen.* **Soriya**'s *making breakfast.* **Marcus** *enters from outside carrying a box.*

Soriya   That was quick.

Marcus   Nah, this is the last of what was in my car.

Soriya   Oh, then where the hell have you parked your car?

Marcus   Over on the red route. Not risking it after last night.

Soriya   'Cause god forbid anything happen to your baby!

Marcus   Shut it you! You making breakfast?

Soriya   Yeah, but don't panic, there's enough for all of us.

Marcus   No. I was thinking we could go out to eat.

Soriya   Oh. Where?

Marcus   How about the French café by the bridge you always stare into?

Soriya   But what about this?

Marcus   Keep it for George.

Soriya   You say that like she won't insist on coming with us.

Marcus   OK, then put a plate over it. I'll have it for lunch.

Soriya   OK.

Marcus   Sorted! And then I can go straight from breakfast to grab the last few boxes. Sort out everything here. Clean

the place from top to bottom and then before you return
from work hunt down the most beautiful roses for your
bedside table.

Soriya   Aw . . . lilies.

Marcus   What?

Soriya   I like lilies, not roses.

Marcus   Why piss on it?

Soriya   'Cause you're being too cute.

Marcus   I know!

Soriya   Alright! You're not that cute.

Marcus   Well that's just simply not true.

Soriya   Fool! We gonna jump in your car then, if you're
shooting straight off after?

Marcus   Well, since they've locked off the entire road, no.

Soriya   They've blocked off the road?

Marcus   Police tape all the way down to the Westbridge
estate.

Soriya   From last night?

Marcus   Must be.

Soriya   Welcome to Battersea, eh?

Marcus   Ha!

Soriya   Oh hun. We can't go out for breakfast. If they've
closed the road, the whole bridge will be chokka. It'll take
you twice as long to drive anywhere.

Marcus   You think?

Soriya   Yeah, you'll want to get started now whilst the roads
are quiet.

Marcus   Ah man. Ok, we'll just have to do breakfast there at the weekend.

Soriya   It's a date. Do you reckon you'll be all in today?

Marcus   Can't see why not.

Soriya *smiles*.

Marcus   What?

Soriya   Nothing.

Marcus   Weirdo!

Soriya   Weirdo yourself!

Marcus *goes to kiss* **Soriya***, but stops on hearing* **George** *enter*.

Marcus   Ah, look who's up.

George   Well there's an image I don't need before breakfast.

Soriya   Morning to you too!

George   How do you look like that?

Marcus   She didn't twenty minutes ago.

Soriya   Oi!

George   No shouting. Head hurts people.

Marcus   I wonder why?

George   Hey! We tried to come home, didn't we Si? No taxi would drive this way. So we just had to stay –

Marcus   And drink?

George   . . . right.

Soriya   Here!

Soriya *gives* **George** *a plate of breakfast*.

George   I love you.

Marcus   Ah, man. That does look . . .

George   Good! Are the sausages —

Soriya   Grilled not fried.

George   And the tea?

Soriya   Fennel 'which helps suppress the appetite'.

George   Not that that's why I drink it.

Soriya   Of course.

Marcus   You do know you guys are defeating the point of a hangover breakfast?

George   Well, when you do it as often as we do —

Soriya   Did!

George   Right . . . you have to start making cutbacks. Want some?

George *offers* **Marcus** *some of her tea.*

Marcus   Share the tea but not the food eh?

George   Drink the tea, you won't need the food, eh.

Marcus   I'm cool, I'm gonna get going.

Soriya   Let me quickly make you something to take with you?

Marcus   Nah, I'm good. I just remembered there's stuff in storage at my mom's I need to grab as well. I just wanna get in. Then, I'll eat.

George   Isn't your mom's just over on the estate?

Marcus   Yeah, but I need to do one more trip to the old place.

George   That's handy though.

Marcus   True.

George   Well at least there's one benefit to having that eyesore as our view.

Soriya   George!

George   What? Marcus knows I'm kidding! The architecture's clearly stunning.

Marcus   Like an ant farm?

George   I never said that!

Soriya   Busted!

George   You helping Marcus pack today?

Soriya   No. Took a bit of lieu time this morning but should really be hitting the office soon.

George   Why? What did the office ever do to you?

Marcus   Ha!

Soriya   Did you just laugh at that?

George   He can't help that I'm a comic genius.

Marcus   And, I'm gone. Call you later.

Soriya   Make sure.

Marcus   See you.

Marcus *exits*.

George   Bye!

Soriya   OK, genius –

George   You can call me George.

Soriya   Right . . . the bank called again for you this morning, George.

George   What?! They're completely abusing the fact they have my direct line —

Soriya   That you never answer.

George   That they shouldn't expect me to answer, since I could be at work.

Soriya   They write your monthly statement. I think it's fair to assume they know you don't work!

George   It's harassment! No? Bullying! I could probably sue!

Soriya   I doubt it.

George   Well, little Miss Public Relations, had you chosen a proper Indian career, like lawyer, we'd probably have a few more answers here, wouldn't we?

Soriya   I told them I'd get you to call them back.

George   No! Shalln't!

Soriya   Why not?

George   They're just badgering me for their overdraft money —

Soriya   You still have your overdraft? George! You left Uni five years ago!

George   Well I wasn't able to ask Mummy or Daddy for anything! I was being independent! Remember?

Soriya   And doing so well!

George   Well once Marcus is all in, I intend to pay them back fully.

Soriya   Good.

George   Though that does remind me . . .

Soriya   No!

George   I haven't even asked you yet!

Soriya   And yet still I feel the answer will be no!

George   But I have a date with one of the football players we met last night.

Soriya   Already?

George   Hey, he had a hot body and spoke four languages.

Soriya   Fair point . . .

George   He wants to meet me at Bluebirds later . . . I'll tell you all the goss . . .

Soriya   You're forgetting, I don't want to know the goss.

George   Fine I won't tell you but obvs I have no intention of letting him pay!

Soriya   Why not, he's probably loaded!

George   I'm an independent woman!

Soriya   Shouldn't you be independent with your own money?

George   I got you a present with my own money.

George *pulls out a wrapped book.*

Soriya   That you clearly can't afford.

George   Love me, bestest bestest frwend in the whole wide world.

Soriya   Fine! Twenty quid till the end of the month when I expect the rest also!

George   Twenty? Babes! That won't even cover a main with tip.

Soriya   Well luckily for you, you're on a diet.

George   Fine.

George *takes* **Soriya***'s money*

George   Now Dad's gone, don't suppose you fancy a tea on the balcony with a cigarette?

Soriya   Oi! And no! I quit!

George   Course you did! And how is that twenty box from last night?

Soriya   Pipe down!

George   He leaves the toilet seat up, you know?

Soriya   Who?

George   Who do you think?

Soriya   He does not! Besides you have your en suite.

George   I'm just saying . . . I saw the toilet seat, up.

Soriya   George, you're still OK with him moving in, right?

George   Of course.

Soriya   OK.

George   Though if you keep smiling manically like that . . .

Soriya   I'm just . . . happy.

George   Good.

Soriya   Can I open the present now?

George   Yes!

Soriya *tears open the package. She's confused. Lights.*

Scene Three

Newsagents. The shutters are still down as though closed. **Marcus** *enters. The shop owner,* **Saghir**, *is sat behind the till watching him.*

Marcus   Hey. You alright?

Ibi (*o/s*)   Oi! Dad!

Saghir *looks off to where* **Ibi** *is.*

Marcus   Was just in the area so thought I'd pop in. Weren't too sure if you were open though.

Saghir *returns his attention to* **Marcus**.

Marcus   Can't believe how dead it is round here.

Ibi (*o/s*)   Dad! Come! Listen!

Marcus   Ain't seen the Westbridge this deserted since everyone thought the Sheerin kids got swine flu.

Ibi (*o/s*)   Hey! *Joldi!* Quick!

Marcus   Remember that? Bless 'em.

Ibi (*o/s*)   Hello!

Marcus (*noticing the paper*)   Ah, is this talking about the trouble last night? Kids eh?

Ibi (*o/s*)   *Abba!* Come!

Marcus   Like they've got nothing better to do with their time.

Ibi (*o/s*)   Dad! Now!

Saghir (*to* **Ibi**)   Damn it boy, some *kala* boy! Wait!

Beat.

Marcus, *unsure how to react, continues to browse the shop.*

Marcus   If you, erm, need to run back quickly, I'm OK to watch the shop for you for two secs.

Saghir *remains seated.*

Ibi (*o/s*)   It's on the news! *Aa ja!* Come! Just look!

Saghir *stands.*

Saghir   I'll be two seconds. Thank you.

Marcus   Cool.

As **Saghir** *exits,* **Marcus** *wanders around the shop and then decides to select a drink.* **Andre** *pulls up on his bike, allows his bike to fall to the floor and enters the shop.*

Andre   I thought that was you! Wa gwarn stranger?

Marcus   Little Andre! Cool?

Andre *clocks the expensive watch on* **Marcus**'s *wrist.*

Andre   Yes, big man! Is that you though?

Marcus   Don't watch me.

Andre *reaches to the neck of* **Marcus**'s *cardigan to check the label.*
Marcus *shrugs him off.*

Marcus   Or touch what you can't afford!

Andre   What? You think mans like me don't own bare
Stone Island already? I was just checking it's real!

Marcus   Wrenk! You're lucky I don't knock you out for that
comment!

Andre   What? You wanna go blow for blow? Come then!

Marcus   Funny!

Marcus *reaches for his wallet to pay for his drink and pulls out his
car keys at the same time.*

Andre   Nah bredrin! That's how you're going on? Coming
back down sides-in a TT blud?! Oh no!

Marcus   It's a car. Standard.

Andre   Nah! Soz mate! Tyrone's' Corsa is 'a car'. That is a
. . . ah . . . I beg you let me ride it?

Marcus   You're not even serious.

Andre   Just around the block?

Marcus   I swear you've started smoking the same stuff
you're selling.

Andre   Yo! That's bait! How can you try reel off facts like
that and how you don't know who's about?

Marcus   Shut up! No one ain't listening! And you think people round here don't know about you and your little mad self already?

Andre   Mans like me is a business man. Standard!

Marcus   Yeah, yeah.

Pointing at his bike.

Marcus   And is that the company car?

Andre   Ah, piss take. 'Low you, man.

Andre *goes to exit and notices they are alone in the shop.*

Andre   Hold on . . .

He picks up two packets of crisps and puts them in his pocket and then reaches for a car magazine. He turns to exit but is pulled back on his hood by **Marcus**.

Marcus   Uh uh.

Andre *kisses his teeth and replaces the magazine.*

Marcus   And the crisps.

Andre *reaches in his pocket and pulls out one of the packets of crisps and chucks them down.* **Marcus** *puts them back in the correct place.*

Marcus   Now gwarn, get!

Andre   Yeah, yeah. In a bit.

Andre *picks up his bike, pulls out the second crisp packet, opens them and starts to eat.* **Marcus** *sees and* **Andre** *smiles a big grin at him before riding off as* **Saghir** *re-enters.*

Andre   Laters!

Marcus   Right. I better shoot but I'll take this and the packet of crisps for the youte.

Saghir   What else did he take?

Marcus   He didn't take anything just the crisps that I said I'd get him.

Beat.

Saghir   Fine.

Silence as they exchange payment and change. **Marcus** *exits and* **Saghir** *stays fixated on him as he leaves.*

Scene Four

At a bus shelter outside the Westbridge estate. **Soriya** *is sat reading a newspaper.* **Andre** *cycles up behind her unnoticed and reads over her shoulder.*

Andre   If it isn't the girlfriend.

Soriya   Oi! Shit.

Andre   Wa gwarn sexy?

Soriya   Are you kidding?

Andre   Ah, what? Did I frighten you?

Soriya   Approach me again like that again, yeah, and you'll understand 'frightened'.

Andre   What?! You're the one caught slipping. You're supposed to know who's near you at all times. You're from south, remember?

Soriya   Well I apologise for lowering my guard on my commute to work.

Andre   Yeah, well let that be a lesson.

Soriya   Can I give you a fashion lesson about wearing hoods up?

Andre   Bruv! What you talking about? Girls love this.

Soriya   Erm, who exactly?

Andre   Well, you for starters. I can see that smile behind your eyes.

Soriya   Oh right . . .

Andre   What? I lie?

Soriya   You see what you need to see.

Andre   I'm shocked you're even travelling to work on your own after last night.

Soriya   Why?

Andre   Are you silly? Look at this dump!

Soriya   Do you know what happened?

Andre   Man like me was in bed sweetheart, week night and all.

Soriya   Course you were.

Andre   But I'll wait with you until the bus comes, though, if you're feeling prang?

Soriya   You know what? I think I've got it.

Andre   You don't normally come this way in the morning, do ya?

Soriya   And who are you? Neighbourhood watch?

Andre   Would you like that?

Soriya   Well since I know you no longer live around here, wouldn't really affect me would it?

Andre   Who told you that?

Soriya   My dad mentioned you'd moved in next door to him.

Andre   Is it? Well luckily for you I've still got my one cotch round here.

Soriya   I'm sorry?

Andre   By the garages, on Westbridge.

Soriya   A garage?

Andre   Nah. Don't get it twisted, yeah. It's cranked off, warm. Got my flat screen TV in there . . .

Soriya   You're doing alright.

Andre   Heated swimming pool. You should come round, you know. I'll give you the tour.

Soriya   Well ain't I lucky?

Andre   You could be.

Soriya   Well I guess I could swing by when you're on your way back from school. Help you with your homework.

Andre   Don't be dizzy, do I even look young enough to be in school, though?

Soriya   Yes.

Andre   I can't help being blessed with this handsome baby face.

Soriya   Oh dear.

Andre   Nah I'm ramping! I ain't even ashamed. I'm in school, rah!

Soriya   Just running a bit late?

Andre   Nah, on a real, if you want me to go, maybe, for you, I will.

Soriya   Gee. Thanks.

Andre   But don't say I didn't warn ya, when I come out all qualified as a doctor and shit and you regret settling for Marcus when you did!

Soriya   So you're gonna be a doctor yeah?

Andre   Why not? It's not just for your firm you know!

Soriya   Alright!

Andre   Or, I wouldn't mind doing what Marcus does still. Running my own ting.

Soriya   Good for you. Might help if you went school a bit more frequently mind —

Andre   Yeah, maybe. Saw Marcus just now.

Soriya   Yeah?

Andre   He's moving in with ya ain't he?

Soriya   Yes dad! Is that OK?

Andre   So you're proper gonna marry him and shit?

Soriya   Mind your own!

Andre   Do you reckon you're gonna get married in a church or a temple?

Soriya   Erm . . . what?!

Andre   What? That must be the first thing you'd think of – two different peoples marrying and that.

Soriya   Well . . . we'll see I guess.

Andre   I think you should get married in a temple. On an elephant and wear a sari thing like that Pussycat Doll video! Fit!

Soriya   OK. Deal!

Andre   So what they saying, then?

Soriya   Sorry?

Andre *indicates towards her newspaper.*

Andre   Talking about last night?

Soriya   Oh right, yeah, kinda . . . it was allegedly to do with some girl getting attacked.

Andre   That all it says?

Soriya   Pretty much. Bag snatch I reckon.

Andre   Weird, ennit?

Soriya   What?

Andre   Just stuff kicks off round here all the time but this . . . just . . . dunno . . . feels different.

Soriya   Does it?

Andre *shrugs. His phone vibrates. He stares at it for a while before deciding to ignore it.*

Soriya   That's not very nice.

Andre   I'll call her back later.

Soriya   A girl? Interesting . . .

Andre   Nah, not like that.

Soriya   Yeah, yeah.

Andre   Ah, look how sad you look.

Soriya   You expect me to believe you don't have a girlfriend? A pretty little face like yours?

Andre   So you're admitting you fancy me then?

Soriya   Don't avoid the question!

Andre   What? Gal? I got a whirl a gal! But someone special? Now that would be telling.

Soriya   OK . . .

Andre   Now you don't avoid my question.

Soriya   Why don't you ask me when you've finished medical school?

Andre   Please! You'll be past it by then!

Soriya   Thanks!

Andre   Anyways, in a bit choong ting!

Goes to cycle home.

Soriya   Oi! School!

Andre   Ah yeah, yeah, 'low me. 'Low me. I'm gone!

Turns and cycles in the opposite direction. Lights fade.

Scene Five

Saghir's *house.* **George** *enters carrying a camera and tripod.* **Ibi** *is sat alone in the living room.*

Ibi   George?

George   Surprise!

Ibi   You are aware it's still morning!

George   Hilarious! Do you plan on giving me a hand?

Ibi   Sorry. (*Stands to relieve her of some equipment.*) What's all this?

George   Well, I've got Marcus constantly in and out the flat and so figured I should give him some space and maybe try to find a productive way to spend my day. Then I thought how better than to sort out my portfolio.

Ibi   I'm sorry?

George   For my modelling.

Ibi   Right. And you need me to . . . ?

George   Well, I need someone with a good photographic eye to take a headshot of me. No make-up, hair scraped back and two side profiles.

Ibi   What for?

George   One of the big agencies may be interested in taking me on for commercials. They just want to see some basic shots, my studio ones were too touched up. Anyway I should have sorted this out ages ago so I'm going to do it today.

Ibi   And I'm . . . ?

George   Gonna be Mario Testino!

Ibi   Of course. You remember I never went ahead with those evening classes, right?

George   But you wanted to. And that want is really half the skill.

Ibi   Right . . . and what makes you think I don't have anything better to do?

George   Please. You're never at the shop on Fridays so we all know you were sat here watching 'Loose Women' and when you heard the door, you changed it to 'Sky News' to style it out. Put MTV on!

Ibi (*indicating the news*)   They're talking about the drama that must have kicked off by yours last night? Over on the estate?

George   Big fucking surprise! MTV!

George *starts putting on make-up.* **Ibi** *starts setting up the camera.*

Ibi   I thought you said no make-up.

George   Yeah. I'm gonna do 'no make-up', make-up. Natural beauty shining through with the aid of Chanel and Mac. Shush!

Ibi   OK then . . . How's everything with you, anyway? Marcus all moved in now?

George   As we speak. And they are so in love!

Ibi   I detect a hint of jealousy.

George   You can't really be jealous of those two. They're a little bit perfect for each other. If anything it's inspiration to go out there and find the same.

Ibi   And are you?

George   Well, I'm dating! It's a step forward!

Ibi   Good! You'll get snapped up in no time. He's coming round here tonight. Gonna meet us for the first time.

George   Marcus? I can't believe she's blagged avoiding that for so long.

Ibi   I think me marrying Umra didn't help.

George   What did that have to do with anything?

Ibi   Dunno. Just got the impression she was worried 'cause I'd chosen such a traditional path her choice seemed more . . . out there!

George   Ha! Is that what you think? Maybe if you guys lived in Pakistan! Your choice is so much more out there than hers! Not even Saghir married of his race let alone going through with an arranged marriage! Freak!

Ibi   Aw! Look at us. Bonding!

George   Besides Si could do whatever she wants. She is the favourite after all.

Ibi   Favourite?

George   Sorry to say! Order's Soriya and me joint first, then you.

Ibi   Oh so even you come before me despite not even being in the family!

George   Not in the family? How dare you! I have my own key?

Ibi   Oh my. What was I thinking?

George   Unfortunately everything you can do . . . I do better. Saghir realises this. I think you need to too. Where is he, anyway?

Ibi   At the shop. Just dropped him off.

George   Already? I thought your uncle did mornings?

Ibi   Well I kinda thought it'd be better if we were all in all day, today, in case there was trouble again. Plus I wanted to do the audit on the Mac rather than hard copy, but as soon as dad saw Facebook, well, he weren't much impressed.

George   Oh, dear.

Ibi   He clearly doesn't trust I can multi-task.

George   Aw! Were you dismissed?

Ibi   Hurts more when it's your own family.

George   Like their style.

Ibi   It was too quiet anyway and there's still two of them so . . .

George   Fair enough. And where's Umra?

Ibi   Upstairs.

George   Wow! You have her on a tight leash!

Ibi   What?

George   I'm joking.

Ibi   Well don't.

George   Oh my god Ibs. Chill!

Ibi   I am chilled.

George   Wow! You've so changed. Si was right.

Ibi   How have I changed?

George   You used to be so fun, and up for a laugh and now . . .

Ibi   What? I'm not interested in you mocking my wife?

George   Mocking her! What the hell? Ibi, it's me! I thought we were friends?

Ibi So did I.

George What's that supposed to mean?

Ibi George man. You only come round when you want something! Internet won't work. Car's failed its MOT. I'm like a stand-in boyfriend to you. But that has to stop. I got married for fuck's sake!

George Yes, I know! I had to watch, remember?

Ibi I just don't think we should be as close as we were. It's inappropriate.

George Inappropriate? For you to have female friends? Are you just making this shit up now? The Qur'an according to Ibi?! And as for 'I only visit when I want something', what about the time when you were having second thoughts about the whole marriage thing? Who got out of their bed in the middle of the night to come talk to you?

Ibi To 'talk'? Really? Face it George, you were just scared you were gonna lose me.

George Lose you?! I never had you! And even if that was true, I still came! Still went to the wedding! Welcomed your 'wife' home! And sat back and watched you play happy families with someone knowing I could have done a hell of a better job!

Ibi You! You think you could have done a better job? Your biggest concern in life is 'does my lipstick match my handbag'! Boy do you know what I'm looking for in a wife.

Beat.

George Right.

George *exits. Lights.*

Scene Six

Newsagents. **Saghir** *is sat behind the counter alone reading the local newspaper.* **Audrey** *enters in her nurse's uniform.*

Audrey   Oh, hi.

Saghir   Hello.

Audrey   You good?

Saghir   Yes. Tired, but you know . . .

Audrey   Yeah . . . I'm surprised you're open to be honest.

Saghir   Well, they don't pay you to close.

Audrey   True . . . Just got to pay a quick visit to one of my old ladies at 33, and she asked me to get some milk.

Saghir   Work as normal, huh?

Audrey   Yeah. I'll just take this. It's only for tea.

Saghir   You must be tired too, no?

Audrey   No, no. I'm fine. Thanks.

Saghir   OK.

Audrey   This today's?

Saghir   Yes.

Audrey   Talking about last night?

Saghir   Barely. Blaming an 'alleged assault'.

Audrey   Well I guess they can only report facts.

Saghir   Right.

Audrey   I'd better take this as well. Find out what actually happened.

Saghir   Look, I need to ask you . . .

Audrey   I just want to pay for this, thank you Saghir.

Beat.

Audrey   Fine. I'll leave it.

Saghir   We have to talk about it at some point.

Audrey   There's nothing to talk about.

Saghir   I wasn't intentionally eavesdropping but —

Audrey   With your face pressed to the window you heard a lot, yeah?

Saghir   I live next door. Come on.

Audrey   What do you want me to say?

Saghir   That's a nice neighbourhood. Quiet, you know?

Audrey   No, I don't think I do.

Saghir   Things like last night . . . they don't know how to react.

Audrey   Last night was a misunderstanding.

Saghir   I have a daughter.

Audrey   What's your point?

Saghir   I just want to understand the truth.

Audrey   I have a feeling if I tell you the truth you'll be terribly disappointed.

Audrey *puts down the newspaper and milk and turns to exit.*

Saghir   Audrey! Your things! Come! Don't be silly.

Audrey   It's fine. I'll tell her after last night you were clearly too stressed to open.

Audrey *exits. Lights fade.*

Scene Seven

Inside an empty garage on the Westbridge estate. **Andre**'s *mobile phone rings as he kicks a ball against the shutter. He answers it.*

Andre   What?!

Yeah well it's not you who had po po at his yard last night is it?!

Sara!! Do you know what your dad said?! Rape! My mom had to hear that!

No, I stuck to the story, but they ain't buying it and I'm wondering if you're thinking about speaking up and telling the truth anytime soon?

Sara!! Your dad tried to kick down man's door? How does he even know where I live?

You know what?! Go suck out!

Marcus *enters.* **Andre** *hangs up his phone.*

Marcus   Someone's in a good mood.

Andre   What you doing here?

Indicating the ball.

Marcus   Could probably hear you from the street with that?

Andre   And? Feel free to leave. Not really up for talking, yeah?

Marcus   What? You're in my cotch asking me to leave?

Andre   Gassed! This ain't been your cotch since you dipped, fam.

Marcus   Erm, please point out what you put in here, then we'll talk.

Andre   Fine. I'll leave.

Marcus   Jeez, what's the matter with you?

Andre *picks up his ball.*

Marcus   Andre!

Andre *goes to exit.*

Marcus   You stole my cotch and couldn't even get a new sofa? Ya tramp!

Andre   Dickhead!

Marcus   Eeediot!

Andre   Prick!

Marcus   Wallard!

They both burst out laughing.

Marcus   Who was on the phone?

Andre   Some stupid gal!

Marcus   You must like her if she's making you screw that hard.

Andre   No gals worth dramz.

Marcus (*messing his hair*)   Aw. It's like the start of a poem.

Andre *shrugs him off, drops his ball and continues to kick it against the shutter.*

Marcus   Oi! You don't know about discretion?

Andre   Huh?

Marcus   How many other people know about this place?

Andre   Don't be silly, no one. This is just somewhere for me.

Marcus   Then why don't you try keeping it like that?

Andre *stops. Then starts to pass the ball from foot to foot.*

Marcus   You not go school today?

Andre   Funny.

Marcus   Ah! Watch when I see ya mom!

Andre   When you see my mom, tell her I said 'hi'.

Marcus   What's going on?

Andre   What? Mom asked me to leave so I left. Rags.

Marcus   What? When?

Andre   Last night.

Marcus   Why?

Andre   What do you mean 'why'?

Marcus   You're sixteen and your mom asks you to leave?

Andre   Yeah . . .?

Marcus   You get a girl in trouble?

Andre   Shut up!

Marcus   Well what did you do?

Andre   You know what . . . 'low you. You sound like leng. You've fully changed you have.

Marcus   And?

Andre   And that means you lose your privileges of talking to me on a lev's.

Marcus   Cool! Good luck at the home!

Andre, *frustrated, takes his ball and kicks it hard.*

Marcus   Oi! What's gwarnin?!

Andre *ignores him and goes back to repeatedly kicking the ball against the wall. Eventually* **Marcus** *intercepts.*

Andre   I can't wait 'til I'm eighteen!

Marcus   Is it? Which part? Paying taxes or losing your summer holiday?

Andre   I just can't wait to leave these sides. It's fucking dry!

Marcus   Ain't nothing wrong with round here.

Andre   Please. That's why you ducked off?

Marcus   – and happily came back!

Andre   Course, now! You're all loved up . . . living with gal . . . earning big money . . .

Marcus   Big money? Where do you see big money?

Andre   Don't panic I ain't looking to rob ya!

Marcus   Listen to you!

Andre   Don't think I ain't capable!

Marcus   I know you ain't!

Andre   Ya dickhead! Mans like me's a sniper!

Marcus   Mans like you is homeless and I'm guessing scared.

Andre   Scared? I'm not a youte. Just gotta get on with shit innit? Look after number one from now on.

Marcus   By living here? I wouldn't recommend it. Gets kinda chilly, still.

Andre   Don't be stupid.

Marcus   Then where are you gonna stay?

Andre   Hostel tonight. Gotta be in at nine.

Andre *shrugs. Starts kicking the ball again.* **Marcus** *pulls out a £20 note from his wallet.*

Marcus   I'm starving. Run chip shop for me and get yourself something?

Andre   Yeah?

Marcus   Chicken and chips and a Rubicon. Get what you're getting and keep the change.

Andre   Sick!

Andre *picks up his bike and goes to cycle off.*

Andre   I never did nothing you know.

Marcus   Look, you better hurry, chip shop closes after lunch.

Marcus *watches* **Andre** *cycle off. Lights fade.*

Scene Eight

Outside the flat. An old Asian lady is carrying bags. **Soriya** *follows.*

Old Lady   You live here?

Soriya   Yes, upstairs. I'll help you if that's OK?

Old Lady   Oi! *Holi!* Slowly! There are eggs in there.

Soriya   Sorry, right. What number are you?

Old Lady   3 – so you're at the top you say? You're the one that moved in the black fellow?

Soriya   Erm yes. Yes I suppose I did.

Old Lady   Huh!

They walk in silence.

Soriya   Right is this you?

Old Lady   I'll have it from here.

Soriya   OK cool. Have a nice day.

Soriya *goes to walk off.*

Old Lady   You know, it's seeing you with him that gives these boys these ideas. You know, the trouble last night?

Soriya   I'm sorry?

Old Lady   Asian girls should be for Asian men.

Soriya   Oh.

Old Lady   But then people see you with him and they want to try for themselves. See what the fuss is about. Why make a fuss? Everyone lived perfectly happily round here together before you young ones try to integrate and confuse things.

Soriya   Right . . . OK . . .

Old Lady   Don't you try just appease me because I'm old . . .

Soriya   I wasn't . . .

Old Lady   I know what I'm talking about.

Soriya   OK.

Old Lady   And now that poor little girl was raped. Three or four times, they are saying.

Soriya   What? Who's they?

Old Lady   Oh . . . of course . . . a little Asian girl gets raped by some black boys – just opposite, on the Westbridge, under your nose . . . I would turn a blind eye too. Hope you have a lovely rest of day.

The **Old Lady** *enters into her flat leaving* **Soriya** *outside speechless. Lights fade.*

Scene Nine

The flat. **Marcus** *is in the kitchen eating chips.* **George** *enters holding her laptop.*

Marcus   Oi! Trouble! You hungry?

George   I can't eat that? Few things you'll need to learn about me if we're to be roomies. No carbs. No dairy. No sugar. I'm allergic.

Marcus   To all three?

George   Had an allergy test done at Neal's Yard.

Marcus   Which means?

George   For starters I'm more sensitive to the vicious side effects of wheat than most.

Marcus   There are vicious side effects to wheat?

George   Oh god yeah! My stomach sticks out and gets all bloated, I become fatigued . . .

Marcus   Right . . . Do you reckon there are starving people in third world countries who have to turn down a loaf 'cause of wheat allergies?

George   I think I see where you're going with this. But it's a real serious problem!

Marcus   Of course.

George   Oh and another tip. Was that you that tried to throw Lily Donaldson in the recycle bin? Because *Vogue* goes on the shelf, only *Grazia* gets thrown. Soriya would most definitely key your car for that!

Marcus   What's the difference?

George *opens her laptop to upload her pictures.*

George   Between *Vogue* and *Grazia*? Oh lord. I want this to work, honest I do . . .

Marcus   Oi! Seriously! Enlighten me!

George   To be honest Marcus, it would seem you were beyond enlightening.

Marcus   If I tell you you're looking painfully thin in those pictures will that help?

George   Wow! The boy learns quick! *Vogue*'s thick, *Grazia*'s thin. Apart from that, how you settling?

Marcus   Good good. All unpacked and about to go to the dad's.

George   Dun dun dun!

Marcus   Serious . . .

George   Well, Soriya's family's so safe! Grew up with them. They're like my second family, since my first was often quite . . . busy.

Marcus   I guess I'm just worried they'll not think I'm good enough for her.

George   You have your own business. That's pretty impressive.

Marcus   Well you know . . .?

George   Oh . . . because you're . . . (*whispers*) black?

Marcus   Wow! You're as direct as Si.

George   Well don't worry, you can totally play that down! You're half white too remember! And you should be proud of that! The other side's just a . . . blip.

Marcus   That's . . . beautiful.

George (*laughs*)   Dude, you're not a new idea to them! She's talked about you for like a year. They know all about you already!

Marcus   Do they?

George   Totes. And she met your folks right?

Marcus   My mom, yeah, last week.

George *hums wedding march.*

Marcus   Think we're just gonna try living together first.

George   That's your thoughts. But what do you think the dad will be thinking? The dad that's literally just watched one child get married . . .?

Marcus   Yeah but that was arranged right?

George   Still an agreed marriage. Everyone will be wondering where this is going . . .

Marcus   Well . . .

George   Dude. I'm totally messing.

Marcus   Ah man. You just mind I don't sprinkle breadcrumbs in your mouth whilst you're sleeping!

Soriya *enters.*

George   Someone's back early! Part-timer!

Soriya   Someone really needn't have bothered today.

Marcus   How comes?

Soriya   They had to let everyone who lived this way leave early to ensure we got home OK.

George   Cushy!

Marcus *gets up to greet* **Soriya**.

Soriya   I'm exhausted!

George   From half a day? Pathetic!

Marcus   What's up?

Soriya   People! People are . . . crazy!

George   Tea?

George *jumps up to put the kettle on.*

Soriya   Did you know that *Asian women were for Asian men only*?

George   Hear hear!

Marcus   Number 3?

Soriya   She said something to you?

Marcus   She mumbled something when I was moving some stuff in the other day.

Soriya   You're joking.

Marcus   No 'thanks' for the fact I waited for her to pass me on the stairs. Her, taking them one at a time, me holding a large box labelled books!

Soriya   Ah babes . . .

George   You should have told her you're not Asian. Your mom's white, with blonde hair! That would have shut her up!

Marcus   Your mom's blonde?

Soriya   Have you only just met George?

George   Don't panic. I told Saghir the same about your mom. Emphasise the positive, remember?

Marcus   . . . thanks.

Soriya   Ignore her.

Marcus   I am.

George   Here!

Soriya   Thank you.

George   Marcus?

Marcus   No I'm gonna hop in the shower before we have to go.

Marcus *exits*

Soriya   Did they say anything on the news about that the girl that was attacked on the Westbridge last night?

George   Babes, you know I don't watch the news!

Soriya   I know! As soon as the words left my mouth I thought, 'Why bother?'

George   So what happened? Anyone die?

Soriya   Girl got raped.

George   Shut up! How do you know?

Soriya   Old lady downstairs told me.

George   Oh, well then it must be true!

Soriya   Oi!

George   Si. Please. She blatantly saw us in tiny little dresses last night and is now playing the prude.

Marcus *re-enters.*

Soriya   You OK?

Marcus   No hot water. Just put the boost on.

George   Oh sorry. I completely forgot! I've just run a bath.

Soriya   Well they're not expecting us for now, so there's no rush.

George   Though you do want to get there quite early.

Soriya   Because . . .?

George   You're meeting me for drinks later, remember?

Soriya   Oh . . . right . . . yeah . . .

George   Marcus got dinner. I get drinks.

Soriya   Yes woman who has no money.

George   You promised! Besides I don't have a date anymore. He cancelled.

Soriya   What?

George   Don't! I'll cry. I'm going to soak myself to a prune then later we are going out.

George *exits.*

Marcus   So the 'I get dinner, she gets drinks' thing. Is that gonna be the arrangement every night?

Soriya   We just need to get her a job or a boyfriend. Or even just a pet.

George (*o/s*)   I heard that!

Soriya (*quietly*)   She'll be fine. She's just a bit lost at the minute.

Marcus   What you looking at?

Soriya   A cook book.

Marcus   What?!

Soriya   I'm making an effort!

Marcus   Oh, stop! *Reggae reggae* recipes?

Soriya   Well, you always say that's what you eat when you and your friends go out.

Marcus   We also eat Chinese and Italian.

Soriya   Well I'd like to learn how to cook it.

Marcus   Do I have to learn how to cook curry?

Soriya   Carry on yeah and you won't have a girlfriend to cook anything for.

Marcus   Sorry. When did you get it?

Soriya   George got it for me. I think she was taking the piss but there's some good dishes in here.

Marcus   Like . . . ?

Soriya   Steak, peppers and tomatoes with ackee and mushrooms.

Marcus   Well I don't like ackee or mushrooms but mmm, sounds yum.

Soriya   You know what, it's not even for you.

Marcus   Good.

Soriya   Good.

Marcus   So who are you cooking it for?

Soriya   George. That girl has spent most of her life in the Caribbean and slept with most of the cricket teams, she'll get this.

Marcus   Good.

Soriya   Right.

Marcus   Well, I'll leave you to it.

Soriya   Anyhow I cook this, this weekend, and you don't eat any . . .

Marcus   . . . you haven't actually threatened me yet.

Soriya   Seriously Marcus!

Marcus   Of course I'll eat it, just might make myself a portion of chips to go with it rather than the ackee.

Soriya   Then it's just steak and chips.

Marcus   What's wrong with that?

Soriya   I'm trying to do something nice for you.

Marcus   Si, you don't have to . . . If you wanna cook, cool, but cook something you want to eat.

Soriya   But some of these sound nice.

Marcus   Fine then.

Soriya   And it'd be nice to eat something you grew up eating.

Marcus   What like . . . (*reads*) rice and peas or festivals? Babes, that's not me.

Soriya   What? You don't like it?

Marcus   No . . . cook it. I'll love it.

Soriya   I'm not gonna cook something you don't like.

Marcus   OK . . .

Soriya   So, what would you eat? If you were in a restaurant?

Marcus   Just chicken and rice.

Soriya   Like . . . (*reads*) creamy coconut and mango chicken?

Marcus   No . . .

Soriya   OK, well can you throw me a bone?

Marcus   I don't know, Si, just chicken.

Soriya   You're as clueless as Ibi and dad! (*Continues reading*.) Oooh this actually sounds quite nice.

Marcus   So you've decided?

Soriya   Well you like it don't you?

Marcus   But it's for everyone?

Soriya   Babes, George will pick at whatever I cook her, it's for you.

Marcus   Honestly Si . . .

Soriya   Just say thank you and shut up. It won't be a regular occurrence.

Marcus   . . . thank you.

Soriya   Would you mind if I called your mom to ask her for a bit of help?

Marcus   What?

Soriya   Well, I don't have to.

Marcus   Why do you need to?

Soriya   I don't. It's fine. It actually looks quite simple.

Marcus   No, of course. Yeah call her.

Soriya   Thanks. I've just never made stuff like this before. And George will be hopeless.

Marcus   Si . . . my mom's white.

Soriya   I know. We have met.

Marcus   You're not getting it. My mom's white and my dad left. She didn't cook this stuff. The house I grew up in was as white as George's.

Soriya   Oh hun, no one's house is as white as George's.

Marcus   Seriously.

Soriya   Ok. So your mom would cook . . . ?

Marcus   English stuff. Roasts, spaghetti . . .

Soriya   Spaghetti? Very English.

Marcus   Leave off!

Soriya   OK . . . that's fine.

Marcus   I know.

Soriya   I just assumed . . .

Marcus   I know.

Soriya   So would you rather a roast? On Sunday?

Marcus   Fine.

Beat.

Marcus   I'm sorry. I'm just over being embarrassed about not knowing that world. It's not me and I get that. I just need you to, too.

Soriya   I do.

Marcus   Do you?

Soriya   Marcus!

Marcus   Nah, it's just for me, not having my dad around, I didn't go without, you know? I mean I always just kinda looked at Jamie like . . . I don't know . . .

Soriya   No, I get that. And he felt the same . . .

Marcus   You think?

Soriya   He gave you the lease. To his baby. Of course he did.

Marcus   He just taught me so much, you know? And I'm not even on about work stuff. Like he taught me . . . bwoy . . . how to be a man, I guess. He didn't need to be black to teach me that. I don't know . . . it's like I'm realising what's important and what matters and I'm kinda like 'low all the other stuff.

Soriya   I do understand Marcus.

Lights.

Scene Ten

Front of **Saghir** *and* **Audrey**'s *terrace house.* **Audrey**'s *pottering in the garden.* **Saghir** *is home from work.*

Audrey   Saghir. Hi.

Saghir   Hello.

Silence as **Saghir** *finds his keys.* **Audrey** *continues gardening.*

Audrey   You finished early.

Saghir   They made us close up, just in case.

Audrey   In case what?

Saghir   Same as last night.

Audrey   What?

Saghir   Well people are still angry and no one wants to tell them anything, so what can we expect?

Audrey *returns to gardening.*

Saghir   Looks good.

Audrey   Yeah?

Noticing a hanging basket between their two doors.

Saghir This smells wonderful.

Audrey If it's in your way –

Saghir No, no, I like it. Honestly.

Audrey Right . . .

Saghir Look. About —

Audrey Just so you know, the rosemary and thyme just help yourselves.

Saghir Ah. Yes. Thanks —

Audrey Better than that dry supermarket rubbish.

Saghir Yes.

Audrey And cheaper. I mean there's plenty of it.

Saghir Thank you. I'll tell my boy's wife.

Audrey Oh right? Yeah, she'll love it if she likes cooking.

Saghir Yes. It looks very nice.

Audrey Yeah, well, don't take much does it? Got those bulbs off the high street, dirt cheap and if they take, well . . . it's nice innit?

Saghir Yes.

Audrey You're right. It is so quiet here.

Saghir I only meant people here are more likely to think —

Audrey Yeah. Exactly. It allows you to just think . . .

Saghir It's just how rumours spread —

Audrey Yeah . . . feels a bit like, I don't really belong here . . .

Saghir OK, that's just nonsense —

Audrey   The whole street probably thinks . . . well, I thought I'd make the garden look good you know. Show what kind of neighbour I am.

Saghir   Look Audrey —

Audrey   Though, then I look over at yours. You just pave it over. Kill any sign of life for the extra parking space. And it's the same out the back! But no one will look at you like you're not welcome here.

Saghir   No one looks at you —

Audrey   Though you'll argue a patio can be good too – right?

Saghir   Right . . .

Audrey   Perfect for summer barbecues —

Saghir   Yes —

Audrey   Not that you be eating meat.

Saghir   We eat meat.

Beat.

Audrey   God, it's so quiet.

Saghir   Yes.

Audrey   We're sorry, OK? I'm sorry, about the disruption last night.

Saghir   I just wanted to understand correctly.

Beat.

Audrey   I asked him to leave.

Saghir   Your boy?

Audrey   For the best.

Saghir   Right . . . so he did . . . yeah . . .

Audrey   Saghir, I'm so sorry. I completely forgot, I have left food on the cooker.

Saghir   Right.

Audrey *goes in. Lights fade.*

Scene Eleven

Saghir*'s house.* **Ibi**, **Soriya** *and* **Marcus** *finishing dinner.* **Saghir***'s seat is opposite* **Marcus***'s.*

Soriya   Oi! Big head – pass the bliming rotis!

Ibi   Twenty-seven years of this!

Soriya   Twenty-five! Please don't age me.

Ibi   Wow! Feels so much longer!

Ibi *and* **Marcus** *laugh.*

Soriya (*to* **Marcus**)   Don't laugh!

Ibi   You're such a bully. (*To* **Marcus**.) You see what you could get lumbered with? I say run now, while you still have the chance!

Saghir *enters from the kitchen with more food.*

Saghir   I still can't believe I served you in the shop today. Funny, eh?

Marcus   Yeah.

Soriya   I still can't believe you didn't recognise him, Dad.

Saghir   Ssh, eat the paneer.

Soriya   He has the memory of a fish, don't be offended.

Marcus   It's fine. He was busy.

Soriya   You should have introduced yourself.

Marcus   He was busy, Si.

Soriya   Doing what?

Saghir   Soriya! Less chat more eats, hey?

Soriya   Where was chacha-ji?

Saghir   Doing stock take.

Ibi   That I helped prep!

Saghir   Huh!

Soriya   I told you to introduce yourself.

Ibi   Like your style Marcus, zone her out! Then you can move on!

Soriya   Please! Like he could do any better!

Saghir *exits with more plates.*

Ibi   Modest this one! Stick with me Marcus! I can introduce you to some nice Asian women!

Soriya   Er . . . how exactly? You couldn't even find yourself one! (*To* **Marcus**.) I told you it was arranged, didn't I?

Ibi   Don't say it like that!

Soriya   Like what?

Ibi   Like we're one of those weird Asian couples that had never met until the wedding night!

Soriya   You hadn't!

Ibi   She's such an exaggerator! We'd met! Please don't think we're backward.

Soriya   Why would he think you were backward?

Ibi   'Cause some people do!

Soriya   Who?

Ibi   You!

Soriya   I think you seem like you were *made for each other*!

Ibi   You're such a knob! I'm half Pakistani and proud!

Soriya   I'm half Pakistani and proud. I just didn't feel the need to marry a freshie to prove my loyalty!

Ibi   Oh my god! Shut up! (*to* **Marcus**) She's not a freshie!

Soriya (*to* **Marcus**)   Ask him if she speaks English.

Marcus   Erm . . . I gonna just stay out of it.

Soriya   Or better yet, where she is at this 'family' dinner?

Ibi   She's tired.

Soriya   Often tired, ain't she Ibs? I wonder what I could read into that.

Ibi   Only when you come round sis, read away!

Soriya   It's probably for the best anyway. I mean all the interpreting becomes boring after a while.

Ibi   She speaks English, knobface!

Soriya   Not to me she doesn't, fanny 'ole!

Ibi   Soriya's the only one in the family who thought she was above learning Punjabi.

Soriya   I was too busy getting into Cambridge —

Ibi   Where everyone else in the family managed to get into after learning their mother tongue!

Soriya   Our mom's white! Moron! Do you see why I put off this dinner for so long?

Ibi   She's so easy to wind up! I'll teach you the tricks!

Soriya   And FYI, I did not think you were backward. Just shocked such a beautiful girl actually agreed to marry you!

Ibi   Hurts, Si! Hurts!

Soriya   Only joking, munchkin!!

Saghir (*re-enters*)   Soriya, shhh! You're so loud. She's like this at home, huh?

Marcus   Bubbly is the word I like to call it!

Ibi   Now there's a polite word!

Soriya   Shut up!

Marcus   Saghir. You need a hand?

Saghir (*exits*)   No. No thank you.

Soriya   Ah! You're such a kiss ass! I love you!

Ibi   Kiss ass? How did you get a first?

Soriya   How did you get a wife, 'knobface'?

Ibi   Argh! It's like arguing with a child. God Marcus! You've got your work cut out!

Marcus *gives* **Soriya** *a kiss.*

Ibi   Oh, Dad! Quick! Public displays of affection!

Soriya *kicks him under the table.*

Soriya   And he says I'm the child?

Ibi   Dad! Don't worry about anything else. Think I'm gonna be sick!

Soriya   Jealousy. Pure jealousy!

Saghir (*enters*)   Shhh shhh! You're all so loud!

Soriya   Isn't my dad adorable? Forgetful, but adorable!

Soriya *grabs and wiggles* **Saghir**'s *cheeks.*

Saghir   Get off!

Ibi   Dad! Sit down! Come on. Relax! Before it all gets cold.

Saghir   Yes yes! Everything OK?

Soriya   Perfect.

Saghir (*to* **Marcus**)   How you getting on?

Marcus   It's amazing, thank you. You're a talented cook.

Soriya   Ha! Don't be fooled! This is the work of Miss Pakistan! These two don't know where the kitchen is!

Saghir   Soriya! Ssh! Everybody, eat! Please.

Saghir *serves* **Marcus** *more food on to his plate.*

Marcus   Thank you.

Saghir   So . . . erm . . . well . . . how you finding living in the flat then Marcus? With George and her silly dieting.

Ibi   Ha! She's a nightmare. She sticks pictures of Abercrombie models on the biscuit tin then asks you *if you think they eat biscuits* when you try and get one.

Marcus   That could probably be useful!

Ibi   I mean it's the ultimate girlie flat! They read fashion magazines and watch programmes about next top models. You sure you can handle it?

Soriya   How would you know, Ibs? I can't remember the last time you came over to visit *me*?

Ibi   Funny.

Saghir   Soriya shh.

Marcus   I have enough box sets of *The Wire* to balance things out.

Ibi   Nice.

Marcus   And literally just got the last of my stuff in today, but very happy. I used to live on Westbridge as a kid didn't I, so the area's home really.

Ibi   Oh my god, did you guys hear that a woman got attacked right by yours yesterday, over on that Westbridge?

Marcus   Attacked?

Ibi   Yeah. They mentioned it briefly on the news earlier.

Saghir (*serves* **Marcus**)   You eat fish?

Marcus   Thank you.

Ibi   What happened again?

Soriya   They just said 'alleged attack of a female'.

Marcus   Like rape?

Soriya   Well . . .

Ibi   Awful, innit?

Soriya   If it happened.

Ibi   They saying who the girl is?

Soriya   Not on the news.

Ibi   Someone 'round here will know. Dad, come on. You're usually good for the details. Did you find out who it was?

Saghir   Erm . . . Ashan's daughter Sara. Let's eat now, huh?

Soriya   Sara?! She's like sixteen!

Saghir   Yes. Roti?

Ibi   Was raped?

Saghir   Attacked.

Ibi   Which means?

Saghir   Pass me a glass please.

Soriya   Attacked by who?

Saghir   Possibly one of the little boys from that estate, Ashan said. Glass.

Ibi   They don't know who?

Saghir   They're not certain.

Marcus   Do police have anyone?

Saghir   No. They questioned people but . . . no one.

Marcus   Jeez.

Ibi   You know who don't you?

Saghir   No. They haven't proven anything yet.

Soriya   Who was it?

Saghir   Nothing is definite.

Ibi   Dad!

Saghir   I won't say!

Soriya   Anyone we know?

Saghir   No, no! Don't be silly. Now please eat.

Ibi   Textbook round here though ain't it?

Soriya   Not rape Ibi, no.

Ibi   No, I meant trouble happening and no one knowing anything.

Soriya   You sure that's not just you? I mean you don't strike me as the most informed person in our neighbourhood.

Ibi   What you on about? I kept an eye on hash tag Westbridge as soon as I heard the first siren. I'm informed.

Soriya   I don't think married men your age should be on Twitter.

Ibi   Ouch!

Soriya (*to* **Marcus**)   Bet your little groupie friend would know more.

Marcus   Nah, doubt it.

Ibi   You have a groupie Marcus?

Soriya   A male groupie! I pretend it doesn't bother me but . . . I'm keeping a close, careful eye!

Marcus   Ha. Ha. Ha. Funny! No, one boy I used to mind when I was little has decided I've grown up and become his Superhero!

Soriya   Sounds gay, doesn't it?

Ibi   The word 'Superhero' isn't helping!

Marcus   Alright!

Marcus *starts to cough.*

Soriya   OK, don't cry we were only kidding.

Ibi   Told you she was a bully.

Saghir   You alright?

Marcus (*coughing*)   Yeah. Yes. Sorry.

Ibi   That dish has chilli in it.

Marcus (*still coughing*)   Yes it does!

Saghir   Pani?

Ibi   Water?

Marcus   Thanks.

Saghir (*pouring water*)   Soriya! Go get the yoghurt!

Soriya   Is it too hot?

Marcus (*coughs*)   No, no, it's . . .

Saghir   I should have made him a sandwich.

Marcus *shakes his head.* **Ibi** *reaches to get the yoghurt.*

Ibi   Here. Put this on the side. It helps.

Marcus   Thanks.

Soriya   He's being dramatic.

Saghir   You OK?

Marcus   I'm fine. Thank you.

Saghir   You sure?

Marcus   Yes. I'm gonna go refill this, though. Through there?

Saghir   I'll get it.

Marcus   Don't be silly. I've got it. Thanks.

Marcus *exits.*

Ibi   So Dad? What do you reckon?

Soriya   Shut up! And Dad! How can you not recognise him? You look so rude!

Ibi   Si, Marcus didn't seem to care.

Soriya   Dad?

Saghir   Soriya, ssh! I'm eating.

Soriya   Did you serve him today?

Saghir   I can't remember.

Soriya   You're so rubbish!

Saghir   I can't be expected to remember every goddam *Kala* boy that comes into the shop Soriya. Now drop it. I'm eating.

Marcus *re-enters.*

Marcus   Think my mouth has started to calm down.

Soriya   Good. You done sweetie? I'm kinda stuffed.

Marcus   You kidding?! Don't be fooled 'cause I had to top up on a little H_2O. I still haven't tried the fish yet.

Soriya   I'm really tired though, and there's still a bit of unpacking to do.

Marcus   Si, I did it all.

Soriya   You did your stuff hun, but there will be stuff I need to sort to make more room.

Marcus   Oh, OK.

Saghir   Soriya . . .

Soriya   Sorry Ibs.

Ibi   Si, stay and let Marcus finish his plate at least?

Soriya   You've finished haven't you hun?

Marcus   Erm . . . yeah.

Soriya   Plus I've got to go meet George. She's gone to some gallery thing and probably shouldn't travel home on her own with everything that's going on, so . . .

Marcus   Well it was lovely to meet you both.

Ibi   You too Marcus.

Saghir   Yes.

Ibi   And you're gonna need to meet Mom next. Her birthday's next month. You going up Si?

Saghir   Stupid woman! Move all the way to bloody Birmingham! For what?

Soriya   Work Dad! No point asking questions you already know the answer to! Yeah, definitely. Just need to sort out a weekend off so it's worth the travel!

Ibi   Cool, well let me know

Soriya   Right. See you Dad.

Saghir   OK.

Marcus   Thank Umra for the beautiful cooking for me.

Ibi   Will do. See you guys.

Soriya   See you.

Marcus   Bye.

Marcus and **Soriya** *exit.* **Ibi** *pulls out his mobile phone to check his Twitter account.*

Ibi   How nice was he, eh Dad?

Saghir *doesn't answer and instead stands to clear the table.* **Ibi**, *oblivious, plays an uploaded video. We hear the following voiceover while video footage of the Westbridge appears.*

Voiceover   The details of the horrific gang rape of a fourteen-year-old Pakistani girl have been flying through Facebook, and thank god, 'cause no one else wants to talk about it. Calling it an 'attack'. Come correct. No less than seven black, Afro-Caribbean males were said to have been involved in the most horrendous sexual attack ever heard. The victim has failed to come forward due to her fear of being deported for being an illegal immigrant and based on that police are reluctant to investigate further. It's the perfect excuse for them not to care, again. If you care, we're calling for all fit and able bodies to attend a protest at the Westbridge Estate at 9 p.m. tonight to voice our disappointment in our justice system! Follow '@Westbridgeprotest' for all updates. Do not let us down! We cannot let these rapists win! We will not be silenced!

Saghir   Ibi! How can you listen to this bloody stupid nonsense?!

Ibi   They're talking about the attack.

Saghir   Who are? Sara's an 'illegal immigrant'? Come! Talk sense please!

Ibi *silences his phone. Lights.*

Scene Twelve

Bar. **Soriya** *and* **George** *dressed up. Tipsy. Sat on chairs at bar.*

George   Your dad said what?!

Soriya   Yep!

George   Awkward!

Soriya   It was horrible.

George   He has a point though.

Soriya   George. No.

George   Babes. Just because you're doing the dirty with him doesn't mean your dad should be able to pull him out of a line-up before a proper introduction. Fair's fair Si.

Soriya   It was just hearing my dad say that word when Marcus was in the next room.

George   I would have had to laugh!

Soriya   OK. Clearly you're not listening!

George   Oh, lighten up! Ibi must have helped you out?

Soriya   Oh, Ibi thought it'd be an appropriate time to talk about rape.

George   Just in general? Nice.

Soriya   He thought this would be the best time to remind Dad, in case he'd forgotten that, oh, yes . . . Marcus is a black guy, and from the Westbridge estate . . . the same estate where a young girl apparently got raped by lots of black guys . . .

George   Oh, babes.

Soriya   See? Not funny!

George   Ibi's a knob!

Soriya   Ibi is a knob.

George   That's why he had to buy his wife off the Internet.

Soriya   I like that you're clearly over all that though . . .

George   I keep looking at his profile picture of the two of them.

Soriya   Oh. Dear. God.

George   I think she's actually prettier than me which is bloody annoying since I'd bet good money she doesn't wear any make-up.

Soriya   She is younger than us.

George   When did we get so old?

Soriya   When did you manage to get back on to the wife?

George   Fine! I hope Marcus wasn't too pissed we left him all alone on his first official night in.

Soriya   If he's even stayed in.

George   Bless him. So come on then . . . what's he like?

Soriya   Marcus?

George   Yep! In bed?

Soriya   What on earth has made you ask that now, after all this time?

George   Well, for starters, I think it's important we decipher if he's truly worth all this drama, plus, I need to know if this new living arrangement will affect my sleeping pattern.

Soriya   Have you ever heard us before?

George   That bad eh?

Soriya   No!

George   Ooooh! And . . . ?

Soriya   And what?

George   Don't act dumb! He's not black. He's not white. Which way did he luck out?

Soriya   George!

George   What? No one's listening.

Soriya   Shut up!

George   It's huge isn't it? I want measurements!

Soriya   No!

George   Not in inches, just is it . . . (*she makes hand gestures*) . . . here? Bigger?

Soriya   I'm not telling!

George   It's tiny isn't it? God bless his blonde-haired mom diluting the genes pool!

Soriya   His mom's not blonde and he is not tiny!

George   Ah! You lucky bitch!

Soriya   I know.

George   Show off!

Soriya   Well, it's nice to remember I've got someone to show off about.

George   OK. You're not allowed to talk anymore.

Soriya   Even if my dad doesn't see it that way.

George   Bore off!

Soriya   I just saw myself being with him forever, you know?

George   Seriously! Stop talking!

Soriya   Did you see that?

George   What? You shagging Marcus's big dick forever?

Soriya   I really don't think that's what I asked!

George   No! But 'little miss perfect having doubts' was too dull to hear!

Soriya   Oi!

George   Oi yourself! You love him, he loves you! End of!

Soriya   Is it?

George   OK, clearly you've forgotten who you're talking to! You're gonna have to save all this wank Dear Jane rubbish for your emotionally in touch friends who have nothing better to do than over-analyse unnecessary things. Me? I'd rather live a little.

Soriya   George! This is my life . . .

George   – that is wonderful! So stop fretting! Saghir has never managed to fully influence you before and look how proud he is. That's what you need to remember. And if you fuck up, well, at least you can say you enjoyed the ride.

Soriya   Yeah, maybe. Wow. That was quite profound for you.

George   Another mastered skill.

Soriya   Almost as strong as your accessorising.

George   Si!

Soriya   What? I'm kidding.

George   Well don't. He already thinks I'm a bimbo!

Soriya   Who?

George   Ibi.

Soriya   And we're back here.

George   I just sometimes think if I never dropped out . . .

Soriya   He graduated with a third! After contesting!

George   At least he graduated!

Soriya   Don't do this . . .

George   Yeah . . . Well how about getting me a new focus then, eh?

Soriya   Erm, why are we out please?

George   Nice try. You and I both know the only reason you agreed to come out was to get away from those protesting hooligans on our doorstep!

Soriya   Well whatever the reason . . . I'm thinking hot rich banker.

George   Interesting! Seen any potentials?

Soriya   Well him at the other end of the bar hasn't taken his eyes off you since we arrived – wearing a suit . . .

George *turns round to look.*

Soriya   Subtle, George! Subtle!

George   He's white?!

Soriya   Let's broaden the pool a bit eh?

George   Yeah. Fair point! He's kinda cute. Do you think I've lost weight?

Soriya   . . . yes . . .

George   OK. Switch seats with me so I can get eye contact.

George *and* **Soriya** *switch seats.*

George   Can't believe you're pushing me towards a white guy.

Soriya   Your fault! Unfortunately you can't be trusted with anyone else since you accused some poor innocent in a robe of being a terrorist this evening.

George   I didn't accuse him! I was very careful not to accuse!

Soriya   Why don't I believe that?

George   OK! Firstly, you weren't there!

Soriya   Thank god!

George   And secondly, religious people are just freaks! So, I actually had every right to be wary whether he was Muslim, Christian . . . or a fucking Hare-krishna. Besides, it's not like I got off the tube. Now that would have been an accusation.

Soriya   You're so considerate.

George   Right? I didn't even switch seats. Because I understand, I have to be seen to be cool with it!

Soriya   I wish I saw your face when he got off the next stop jamming to his iPod! Oh the guilt!

George   Oh babes – there was no iPod. That was my first clue. Who sits on the tube content with their own thoughts? No *Metro*, no music. It's freaky.

Soriya   But you do see you were wrong?

George   Well . . . he didn't blow up *that* tube, no . . . but, have you caught the news this evening? I mean who's to say what line he went on after.

Soriya   I'm thinking we would have heard.

George   Yeah yeah! OK, I was wrong! I admit it! I'm a terrible person who'll go to hell. Happy?

Soriya   Ecstatic.

George   And it's not a colour thing. It's a religious thing. If the boy on the tube was black or white doing the same thing I still would have freaked —

Soriya   But still remained seated!

George   Dude. Being called a racist is not cool. I'm white. I don't get away with it as easily as you do.

Soriya   I have no idea why Ibi didn't just scoop you up!

George   OK! That's mean!

Soriya   Sorry.

George   Well I was actually thinking about that . . .

Soriya   George . . . No.

George   I just think he needs to know how I —

Soriya   He knows how you feel.

George   No. It's always said in game play. I just need to tell him straight so he can do with it what he will but at least he'll know, for certain.

Soriya   And what do you think he's gonna do? Is he gonna leave her? They just got married!

George   No . . .

Soriya   George, honestly, for your sake . . .

George   You know, I have lost weight. This feels huge.

Soriya   What?

George *makes eye contact, smiles and waves at banker off stage. She then stands to go over to him.*

George   OK then . . . your job's done. See you at home, OK?

Soriya   Please! I'm not leaving you here. After what happened last night?

George   What happened last night? Nobody bloody knows. I've heard so many different versions.

Soriya   Well whatever the truth better to be safe than sorry.

George   Ugh! You're like Mary fucking Poppins you. Right. Back in a bit.

Soriya   George. With Ibi . . . Promise me you won't.

George   I'm going to talk to the banker aren't I? What more do you fucking want?

George *exits. Lights fade.*

Act Two

Scene One

Night. **George** *and* **Soriya** *walking home. Tipsy. Stopped outside Dallas Chicken.*

George   Slow down!

Soriya   Hurry up!

George   I am wearing £700 Jimmy Choo python-skin gladiator heels! They are not designed to be walked in!

Soriya   Course they are! How can they expect you to spend seven hundred quid on a pair of shoes and have money left over to catch a taxi?

George   Ugh! Why couldn't Daddy buy me a flat nearer to the goddam tube!

Soriya   I'm starving!

George   I'm tired!

Soriya   Keep up!

George   Why didn't we catch a cab again?

Soriya   'Cause you couldn't afford one and I didn't want to embarrass you by paying for you . . . AGAIN!

George   This is dangerous you know. You're risking our safety. A girl was raped!

Soriya   Oh suddenly now you're concerned!

George   And there was a protest on tonight.

Soriya   Pipe down! That would have finished years ago!

George*'s ankle gives way and she lets out a scream.*

Soriya   Oh! What now!

George   I think my ankle's broken!

Soriya   You and those goddam shoes! If you don't get up now I'm gonna leave you here!

George   Fuck off! Leave me to get gang raped by all those little shits over there?

Soriya   Shh! Will ya!

George   Well, help me up!

Soriya *tries to pull* **George** *up but* **George** *ends up pulling* **Soriya** *down.*

Soriya   I thought you'd quit the carbs?

George   I'm sorry. Do you not enjoy having a roof over your head?

Soriya   Spoilsport!

Soriya *gets back to her feet.*

George   Sssh! What was that?

Soriya   What?

George   I can't believe they touched a fourteen-year-old girl? It's pathetic!

Soriya   Fourteen?

George   It's all over my BBM!

Soriya   What? Sara's not fourteen!

George   Who's Sara?

Soriya   You're not even trying!

George   I am! Pull harder!

Soriya   I'm too weak! As if Dallas Chicken is the only place open. Come on let's just do it! It'll be our little secret!

George *finally rises.*

George   No! Are you kidding? I want that place closed down! It's a health hazard. They should open a Simply Food M&S but that lot (*points to Westbridge estate*) keeps it in business!

Soriya   You're such a snob!

George   And you're a ghetto queen that brought the hood rat into my bachelorette pad.

Soriya   Marcus is not a hood rat. He's from Clapham!

George   Clapham Junction! There's a difference!

Soriya   And where do you think you live?

George   South Chelsea?

Soriya   Hate to break it to you, SW11, same as those from the chicken-eating estate.

George   Ugh! My parents really really hate me don't they?

Soriya   Luckily you have me!

George   I love you. Even if you are from India!

Soriya   – Africa!

George   How is that again?

Soriya   Do you just never listen to me?

George   Oh! Sorry, yeah. I love you even if you are from Africa!

Soriya   And I love you even if you are from Battersea.

George   South Chelsea!

Soriya   How is that again?

George   I'm divorcing my parents.

Lights.

Scene Two

Outside **Saghir***'s house.* **Audrey** *is next door scrubbing graffiti off her wall.* **Saghir***'s coming home. There are broken bottles all on the floor which have clearly been thrown at the house.*

Audrey   You have fun telling everyone what my boy did?

Saghir   Are you OK? Is everything OK?

Audrey   Gwarn man! Everything's criss. No more than a failure of a mother like me deserves. Eh?

Saghir   Look you should be inside. Leave this for the morning. They might come back.

Audrey   And have everyone round here see this?

Saghir   I'll get my broom and sweep up the glass.

Audrey   No bother with that.

Saghir   Shush!

Saghir *goes inside and returns with a broom and starts sweeping up the broken glass from smashed windows.* **Audrey** *continues to clean. Silence.*

Saghir   That stupid protest should never have been allowed to happen. They didn't even know what they were speaking of. Making up more facts to stir up more hatred, you know? So many stupid Muslim boys being angry but not really sure why.

Audrey   That girl, the one that . . .

Saghir   Sara?

Audrey   Yes. She dropped all charges her dad put against him. Police came round today to tell me in case I wanted to bring Andre home. 'Now why would I want to go and do a silly little thing like that?' I told them! She was probably just scared. Or humiliated . . . just wants to forget.

Silence as they continue to clean.

Audrey   He denied it you know. Over and over, but I could see in his face he was lying. I know my son. Him just like him dad! Tells me he don't smoke weed, when I can smell it. Him went school, when his teachers asking me to bring in his sick note . . . I hear him, at police station saying the same lie over and over. Him was at him *'bredrin's yard'*!

I called up his friend and Andre did come round but must have left about half nine. He didn't get in 'til gone twelve. That's three hours. And your son, your Ibi, outside the shop locking up tells me he did see him with a group of mans . . . so you see? I just know.

Audrey *returns to cleaning the wall. Silence.*

Saghir   I never tell no one about your son. No one's bloody business.

Audrey *pauses. Continues to clean.* **Saghir** *continues to sweep. Lights.*

Scene Three

Outside the flat. **Soriya**'s *being sick.*

George   I told you not to eat that chicken but no! Soriya always knows best! My pores are so blocked from just being in that place! I can actually feel them!

Soriya *gags again.*

George   I'm not even certain it is chicken that they sell! I mean you have to question how they can sell meat for so cheap!

Soriya   Oh my god! Shut up and hold back my hair or something useful!

George   Ah babes! You know I'd love to! But I really don't deal very well with vomit! You know if I get any closer to you I'll end up joining in.

Andre *cycles up.*

Andre   Good night?

George   Shouldn't you be in bed?

Andre   Er . . . Shouldn't you have a job?

Soriya   Oh god. I think I'm gonna die!

Andre   Urggh! I can actually see whole chips in your sick. Did your mother never teach you to chew your food?

George   Ew! Right that's it! I'm going up! Hurry up!

Soriya   I'll follow.

George *hesitates.*

Andre   It's cool. I'll wait with her until she done.

George   Si! Be quick!

Soriya   I will.

George *exits.*

Soriya   Tell me you have a tissue or something on you?

Andre *pulls out a screwed-up piece of tissue and hands it to her.*

Andre   I swear on my life it's clean.

Soriya   Thanks.

Soriya *goes to walk and then decides to sit instead.*

Soriya   Now I'm reckoning that that lamp isn't moving, it's just me drunk, but I still feel the need to check . . .

Andre   It isn't moving! Hadn't you better go inside now?

Soriya   Ugh! Not until my stomach stops churning. I don't know if Marcus is up there or not and if he is, best he doesn't see me like this.

Andre   Must be nice to have someone waiting for you though.

Soriya   How comes you're out this late?

Andre   What you expect me to miss the action? It's all kicking off. I knew it would from when some dickhead tried to broadcast that stupid message on BB.

Soriya   Will your mom not be wondering where you are?

Andre   I don't live at home.

Soriya   Oh. So where do you live?

Andre   At one hostel. It's cool though. No one to nag me . . .

Soriya   You don't get a curfew?

Andre   Long gone. You just clock in and show your face and then dip off, after hours, when it'd be rude for them to knock your door. You alright?

Soriya   Yeah. The fresh air's helping.

Andre   Look, I've gotta dip. You better go in. Peoples are still carrying on nutty trying loot up people's house and that.

Soriya (*to herself*)   Shit! Dad's shop.

Andre   What?

Soriya   Nothing. Where you going?

Andre   Gotta go buck my bredrin.

Soriya   You know what people round here are saying?

Andre   What?

Soriya   The girl that was attacked, was raped, was gang raped by some kids off that estate.

Andre   What do you reckon?

Soriya   I asked Marcus if he could guess who it might be, you know, 'cause he lived there.

Andre   Time ago!

Soriya   I know, but still. And then I thought, if anyone's gonna have answers, it would be you. But Marcus made me promise not to ask.

Andre   Answers to what?

Soriya   To who did it.

Andre   So you ra think it happened?

Soriya   He said, some shit just kicked off at home and you had to leave. Why would your mom make you leave home Andre?

Andre   So if you knew I wasn't at home already, why ask? Kinda snidey, ennit?

Soriya   Curious to what you'd say.

Andre   What are you getting at?

Soriya   Just odd isn't it? You get kicked out the same night a girl got raped on the estate.

Andre   Are you serious?!

Soriya   Look, I'm just asking . . .

Andre   No you're not! You're accusing! You dizzy little bitch!

Soriya   Erm, excuse me! Watch your mouth!

Andre   Nah! You watch yours! True say I thought you was cool but now? 'Low you man! You're as dumb as that stupid little flat mate of yours. Chasing after black man and Indian man like she don't see what goes. How long have you known me for now, eh? And what about Marcus? He used to babysit me when I was a youte.

Soriya   That was a long time ago. People change!

Andre   Ah, seen. There you go again. You know what, fuck you!

Soriya   I'm not saying it was you. But I do find it hard to believe when you're out here night in night out that you don't know more than the scraps of information they're feeding us.

Andre   Soz babes. I don't associate with rapists. Not my style ya get me?

Soriya   So a girl was definitely raped? Well that's something.

Andre   Shut up! How many times have you cut through the estate late at night? Huh? And how many times have you felt scared? Never! You really think you could be walking through estates in Bow or Hackney with that same feeling of ease? These streets don't belong to no rapists.

Soriya   That's a very sweet outlook hun but unfortunately . . .

Andre   Don't 'hun' me! The reason you don't know nothing is 'cause there's nothing to know. You think some little girl got raped? Where is she then? The girl don't exist. It's just a story some messed-up person started so they could cause a lot of dramz.

Soriya   People don't make up stories like that! Not about rape. It's too . . .

Andre   Shut up man! Yes they do. They hear a little something and retell it to suit their needs. 'Cause if a young Asian girl gets raped by a young black boy or worse, boys, then all Indian people round here have ammunition to say what they really think about their black neighbours! They can say they hate the way man like me smoke weeds on street corner, not thinking about the fact I ain't causing no harm to no one . . .

Soriya   Don't flatter yourself darling, no one cares that much.

Andre   That little blonde thing upstairs has proper rubbed off on you. And it's vice versa! Don't get it twisted. You think black women round here, hard-working black women want to see one of the few sharp, intelligent, and I'll ra say it, handsome, black men shacked up with a paki?

Soriya   Oi!

Andre   Ah. Did that sting? Don't pretend you haven't clocked on to that any ways. They would all love to see you married off to some distant cousin from back home. Then they'd be happy for you.

Soriya   You know what you're boring me now . . .

Andre   Ah. My bad. You want entertainment. Shame, 'cause I only deal with facts, like Indian girls like cock same as everybody else! Black cock even. But then you already know that, don't you? Yet when I say it, you're thinking even more I did it, aren't you? How about if I put my hood back up, like how I know you love it. Does that fuck with your head even more? Are you now certain I did it? How about if I step towards you in a way and walk just standardly how black guys walk? Now what you thinking?

Soriya   Get away from me.

Andre   You so think you're a part of this here world. And yet you wanna make those sorts of comments. And you think making them with a black man on your arm makes it OK? You can't be racist, can you, if you're fucking him at night? He ain't even black sweetheart. You need to realise. One baby with you and that gene's gone!

George *re-enters.*

George   Oi! What's going on?

Andre   Silenced.

Soriya   Hey George. Go back upstairs.

George   Si?!

Soriya   I just need to swing by my dad's, quickly! Get back inside. I'll call you when I get there.

Soriya *turns to exit.*

George   Oi! Si! Don't be silly. You've been drinking you can't drive!

Soriya *exits.*

George   Si! Get in! It's dangerous! Si! Come on! I'll call you a cab! (*To* **Andre**.) What the hell?

Andre *shrugs his shoulders.*

George   You were supposed to be looking after her! Excellent bloody job!

Andre   She's too . . . drunk.

George   Yeah, she is!

George *turns to exit and hears a commotion coming from the direction* **Si** *went.* **George** *tries to call* **Soriya**. *No answer.*

George   Well now what you gonna do?

Andre   What?!

George   I swear if anything happens to her . . .

Andre   How is this my fault?

George   She has to be in her car by now. The red route's only there. Quick! Come upstairs! See if we can see her.

Andre *follows reluctantly behind* **George**. *Lights.*

Scene Four

Saghir*'s living room.* **Saghir***'s sat reading a newspaper.* **Ibi** *enters.*

Saghir   Hello?

Ibi   Just me.

Saghir   Where's Umra?

Ibi   She stayed at Amira's.

Saghir   You not supposed to stay overnight?

Ibi   I saw the news and thought I'd better check you were OK. Have you just got back from the shop?

Saghir   No, they made us close earlier.

Ibi   Is it?

Saghir   . . . it is.

Ibi   Nah, I was calling. Seen next door's house?

Saghir   Yes. We cleaned up most but then figure save the rest for morning.

Ibi   And all down the high street, over to Westbridge? There's kids and police everywhere. You pulled the shutters on the shop yes?

Saghir   Of course. Ask me stupid bloody questions.

Ibi   OK. Cool.

Saghir   Waste of bloody time coming back, hey?

Ibi   Well no, it's fine. Peace of mind knowing you're alright.

Saghir   Yes, yes. And you'll pick Umra up in the morning?

Ibi   Well no, she wanted to stay with Amira tonight as they're going to some market in the morning but I said I'd go meet them in the evening for food plus I've got us tickets to see *The Lion King* tomorrow so we still get to do something nice.

Saghir   *Lion King*?

Ibi   Yes.

Saghir   Who do you think she is? American tourist? Don't be stupid! Rubbish show, plus Alijan and the boys are coming over from Greenford tomorrow. They want to meet the lovely Umra. So do they come here or do we all go to Amira's?

Ibi   Dad! No! It's booked!

Saghir   Ibi. Umra wants to see family. Not silly Disney shows she won't even bloody understand! Why do you think she's always with Amira, huh? *Lion King*? Ha!

Saghir *is engrossed in the paper.*

Ibi   Fine I'll see if I can sort a refund.

Ibi *goes to exit as* **Soriya** *enters.*

Ibi   Hey sis!

Saghir   Soriya?

Soriya   Hey Dad? Can I crash here tonight?

Saghir   It's after bloody midnight. What are you doing out?

Ibi   You look a fucking mess sis.

Saghir   Ibi!

Soriya   Thanks! I'm tired and I just wanna go to bed.

Saghir   You OK?

Soriya   Yeah, I'm fine Dad. Just tired.

Saghir   You shouldn't be out driving with all these idiots about!

Soriya   Dad . . .

Saghir   I'll go upstairs and make up the bed.

Saghir *exits.*

Ibi   What's up?

Soriya   I told you. I'm tired.

Ibi   And I'm telling you knobface, you're lying.

Soriya   Do you think everyone hates the fact that me and Marcus are together?

Ibi   Who's everyone?

Soriya   Neighbours? Friends?

Ibi   Insignificants you mean? Why would you care?

Soriya   Just an old lady said something to me tonight, about how maybe we don't belong together.

Ibi   People have been saying that for years! And there's a word for them!

Soriya   Sensible?

Ibi   Have you and Marcus had a fight?

Soriya   No. Just since Sara was . . . people have been a lot more forthcoming with their opinions on mine and Marcus's relationship. I'm getting tired of defending it.

Ibi   Well don't. I don't defend me and Umra to anyone.

Soriya   Yeah, but you're weird . . .

Ibi   I know.

Soriya   I wish I was as confident about me and Marcus as you are about you and Umra.

Ibi   Yeah, but that was easy for me. Everyone around us were splitting up, divorcing. Mom and Dad, friends from Uni. The only people I knew in long stable relationships were those that married for practicality rather than love. The love will come and I just have to trust that.

Soriya   You don't think Mom and Dad should have got married do you?

Ibi   I think Mom made a lot of sacrifices to be with Dad. How could you not eventually be bitter when you see it's not being returned?

Soriya   When you told me you were marrying her, I was so worried for you.

Ibi   And now?

Soriya   I don't know. She's obviously beautiful and sweet and kind but . . .

Ibi   Sounds like an alright package to me.

Soriya   Where is she?

Ibi   Amira's.

Soriya   You see?

Ibi   What? She not allowed to have friends now? You moved your boyfriend in with your best friend. Could have got your own place but, no.

Soriya   That's different.

Ibi   Is it?

Soriya   You're married.

Ibi   So we have to spend every waking minute together?

Soriya   Newly married.

Ibi   I'm just giving her her space. She's a lot younger than us. I can't even imagine how overwhelming it must be. Like going to study abroad but having to lodge with a family.

Soriya   She did agree.

Ibi   I know and like me she knows she's made the right choice. That doesn't mean you don't get scared from day to day. It's a journey, like any other. I guess I just want to iron out a few of the pot holes for her.

Soriya   Make sure she knows how lucky she is.

Ibi   And how lucky I am. She makes me feel safe and loved and I can't wait to start a family with her.

Soriya   It sounds almost perfect.

Ibi   Nothing's perfect Si.

Soriya   I get told me and Marcus are.

Ibi   That's a lot of pressure.

Soriya   Yeah. I feel like I've been so happy with Marcus as long as others have been happy for us.

Ibi   And now?

Soriya   I just want to be happy for myself.

Ibi   Makes sense.

Soriya   Dad didn't love him, did he?

Ibi   Dad will love whoever you love.

Soriya   He loves Umra.

Ibi   God! You sound jealous!

Soriya   No. Just happy to see you so . . .

Ibi   Yeah.

Soriya   I'm sorry for always being a dick!

Ibi   Please, I'm used to it!

Ibi *hugs* **Soriya** *and makes his way up to bed.*

Soriya *is left alone on the sofa. Lights fade.*

Scene Five

The flat.

Sound of crowds of people below.

Andre   She answering her phone yet?

George   No! Do you think it's too late to call the landline?

Andre   Not if you're stressing.

George   I'm just scared 'cause if she hasn't gone there then I'll cause them to panic.

Andre   'Low it then! How pissed was she?

George   Well she was sick . . .

Andre   You girls man . . . and you wonder why things happen.

George   Yes child!

Crowds get closer. **Andre** *spots a bag of weed on the table. Smirking, he picks it up and shakes it in front of her.*

Andre   Tut tut tut!

George   Put it back.

Andre   Girls like you make me laugh yeah.

George   I'm not the same customer as the little skag heads you sell to on the estate, yeah?

Andre   Er . . . actually love . . . you are.

George   Put it back.

Andre   If you think I'm looking to rob you why invite me into your house?

George   Because it's manic out there.

Andre   Please! I'm a big man. Anyways, I betta dip.

George   What?

Andre   I've gotta go.

Andre *turns to exit. We still hear the shouting outside.*

George   No. Wait. Stay with me please. Just until Marcus or Si comes back?

Andre   You'll be fine. How many floors up is this?

George   It's not that. I'm just scared.

Andre   Oh, OK.

Andre *is shocked by the request for help but agrees to stay. Sound of breaking bottles and shouts happen louder.* **Andre** *sits down opposite* **George**. *They have nothing to talk about. Suddenly a brick comes through the window.*

Andre   Shit! You OK?

George   Erm . . . yeah.

Andre   Nah they're taking the piss!

Andre *exits. Lights fade.*

Scene Six

Outside **Saghir**'s *house.* **Soriya**'s *smoking.* **Marcus** *enters.*

Soriya   Fuck!

Marcus   Whoa! Sorry to scare you? What's up?

Soriya   Nothing. I'm fine.

Marcus   And smoking again apparently . . .

Soriya   I never said I'd quit, I said I'd cut back. And I have!

Marcus   OK. George called. Said you were upset? You OK? You coming home?

Beat.

Marcus   Si. . . . ?

Soriya   I don't think this is a good idea.

Marcus   What?

Soriya   Me and you?

Marcus   What?!

Soriya   I want out.

Marcus   Are you serious?

Beat.

Marcus   Look. What's up?

Soriya   Nothing.

Marcus   You're OK?

Soriya   Yes. No. I don't know!

Marcus   Look, you're starting to freak me out here.

Soriya   I'm sorry it's just . . .

Marcus   Just what?!

Soriya   Do Asian people and black people belong together?

Marcus   What?

Soriya   Name one successful mixed-race couple.

Marcus   There's loads!

Soriya   Name one! Someone with a successful marriage under their belts.

Marcus   Are you fucking kidding me?

Soriya   No. I need you to help me 'cause I have all these thoughts swimming through my head and I desperately want you to stop them.

Marcus   If two people love each other that's enough.

Soriya   Really? 'Cause my parents loved each other and they couldn't make it work. I'm guessing your parents did and they didn't manage to stick it out . . .

Marcus   We're not my parents or your parents. We're different.

Soriya   Why are we? What makes us so special? Everything we have in common is in line with our age. We like the same music, the same films, but that's it. We've grown up in completely different cultures, different worlds and I just worry they don't mesh together all too good.

Marcus   Ah for fuck's sake! My mom loves you and your dad likes me. They're our worlds! Meshing!

Soriya   No. Our parents are respecting our choices. I'm sure if they could make the decision for us they wouldn't wish this.

Marcus   Wish what? Us to be happy? God forbid!

Soriya   I'm not like you, OK? I'm not cool with who I am! I grew up my whole life being so grateful I was raised with my dad. People stare at me when they can't place where I'm from. They know I'm not white but after that they get stuck. When I'm with my dad they understand. We're Asian. I have an identity. And I love it. I love everything that comes with it. I love belonging to a large family that bickers over the dinner table. I love getting dressed up to go to our many relatives' weddings. I love Dad forcing us to watch crap soaps on ARY when we have dinner round his despite all the protests to just put *EastEnders* on . . .

Marcus   And nothing will change that.

Soriya   I'm scared you'll change that.

Marcus   Are you taking the piss?

Soriya   No I'm upset 'cause I've just realised I don't think mixing races works.

Marcus   What?

Soriya   I know it's a horrid thing to say, but it doesn't mean I can stop thinking it.

Marcus   And if we were to last and go the distance . . . you don't wanna find out? It shouldn't be about colour or heritage but love and compatibility outside of 'our dads were raised in the same city'. It's a weak link!

Soriya   I'm gonna have an arranged marriage.

Marcus   Oh my fucking god?! What the fuck?!

Soriya   Not right away but it's what I want. I want to have Pakistani children for a Pakistani husband. I don't want my children to be as confused as I am.

Marcus   You're underestimating yourself completely. You'd be an amazing mom. You don't think I see that in you? Why do you think I wanna be with you?

Soriya   I'm sorry.

Marcus   And what about your mom? When your children see she's white? They'll know they're mixed and you'll still have to explain to them. Your neighbours' comments have got through . . .

Soriya   Don't be stupid. Just things are different now.

Marcus   Now what? Now some girl got raped?

Soriya   It's got nothing to do with her.

Marcus   I find that hard to believe. We were fine. Better than fucking fine. Great. And then some nigger rapes a paki and suddenly —

Soriya   A what?

Marcus   You know what I mean?

Soriya   A paki?

Marcus   Fuck off! I didn't mean it like that! George says it all the time!

Soriya   It's not the word it's the tone, the context! Everyone knows that!

Marcus   Same as nigger?

Soriya   Exactly!

Marcus   But me saying that didn't offend you!

Soriya   You didn't say nigger.

Marcus   Yeah I did.

Soriya   Well I wouldn't hear that, would I, it's not offensive to me.

Marcus   It's not offensive to me either.

Soriya   Well good for you.

Marcus   'Cause I know I'm not that. Some wasteman that hangs around the estate doing all sorts with girls, now *that* accusation seems viable. Same way you're not a paki.

Soriya   That word shouldn't be used to describe anyone.

Marcus   I know and I'm sorry. It's just. I'm angry. I can't help but think about some young girl, your dad's friend's daughter, who's sat at home, whilst all this is going on and refusing to come forward.

Soriya   She might be scared.

Marcus   She might be exaggerating!

Soriya   How can you say that? She was raped. Gang raped.

Marcus   We don't know that. It just said 'attacked'.

Soriya   To be honest, that's not even the issue anymore.

Beat.

Soriya   How could we ever have thought this could work?

Marcus   This what? We were made for each other!

Soriya   Erm – I think a lot of people would disagree with that. If we were really made for each other wouldn't you be Asian or me black or anything other than Asian?

Marcus   What kind backward talk is that?

Soriya   Backward? What do we even have in common?

Marcus   We . . . we . . . like the same music, films . . .

Soriya   We're so different and you don't see it!

Marcus   And you do?

Soriya Yes!

Marcus Since when?

Soriya Since now!

We hear sirens in the distance.

Marcus God! Tonight's ridiculous. Please can I get you home, safely? George is alone in the flat. We should go back, check she's cool and then talk.

Soriya I'm gonna stay here tonight. We can talk some more in the morning. Fresh.

Marcus OK. Well can I stay here with you?

Soriya No. You should check on George. Tell her I'm sorry for running off. I'll be home in the morning.

Marcus Soriya . . .

Soriya Night.

Marcus What I said about the girl . . .

Soriya It's not even the issue anymore.

Soriya *exits into the house. We hear more sirens. Lights.*

Scene Seven

Outside the Westbridge. **Andre**'s *walking alone pushing his bike alongside him.* **Audrey** *runs in from her parked car.*

Audrey Oi!

Andre *sees his mom and stops.*

Audrey There's a riot going on and you just feel to up and walk street? Like you have no home!

Andre I don't.

Audrey Even if you did you'd still be out here. Like some sort of street urchin! You know how many people have ended up in hospital tonight 'cause of it. They've smashed out next door's shop! You want to see the front of the house!

Andre   And?

Audrey   I dunno what is the matter with you.

Andre   What you doing here?

Audrey   They call me up as soon as they seen you never show. Threatening to kick you out.

Andre   Is it?

Audrey   And then what you gonna do? 'Cause I can't take you back.

Andre   No one asked you to.

Audrey   You don't see Andre. What you putting me through. I'm too old for this shit. I shouldn't be sat in my car in the middle of the night, waiting for you to stroll by.

Andre   No one asked you to!

Audrey   Actually darling they did. Saying if I never come down here and find you quick them a call the police. 'Cause you can't stick to no curfew? How hard is it?

Andre   I had things doing?

Audrey   I hate this estate – and yet I knows it's where you would be. What I don't understand is why you like it so much? It's ugly, and full of all sorts.

Andre   It's home. Ain't full of nothing but family.

Audrey   These people ain't your family. You think you're gonna be able to rely on them? Which of them would have noticed if you never reached your bed tonight?

Andre *shrugs*.

Andre   They know I didn't rape no girl. Not 'cause they was with me all night just 'cause they know. The way family do.

Beat.

Audrey   I wish I could know. I really do. But your dad had a gift for lying –

Andre   I'm not my dad!

Audrey   I know!

Andre   I'm not like him.

Audrey   Andre . . .

Andre   I hate him!

Audrey   I know.

Andre   But then I hate you for seeing him in me!

Audrey   I know.

Andre   Mom. Go home!

Andre *gets on his bike and cycles off.*

Scene Eight

George *alone, drunk. The window is broken.* **Marcus** *enters.*

Marcus   You know there's still people down there? (*Seeing the window.*) You OK?

George   Fucking fantastic! You?

Marcus   What happened to the window?

George   You know I hadn't noticed!

Marcus   Shit! Are you OK?

George   I'm fine. I'm off to bed.

Marcus   George. I'm so sorry. You weren't injured though right?

George   No.

Marcus   Cool. Go to bed. I'll have it all cleared up by morning.

George   Don't be silly. It's not your fault. Just wanted to rant.

Marcus   Honestly. It's the least I can do.

George   I've arranged for someone to come out first thing tomorrow. It'll be fine tonight . . . so long as it doesn't rain again!

Marcus   OK, well I'll at least clear up all this so you or Soriya don't end up cutting yourself.

George   Where is Si?

Marcus   Dad's.

George   And why couldn't she call me?

Marcus *shrugs*.

George   You needed to see how she stormed off earlier and just left me alone! Jumped in her car, drunk, and left me! I think she accused Andre of attacking that girl.

Marcus   Andre? What?

George   I know!

Marcus   When did she see Andre?

George   Oh he was passing, as usual.

Marcus   And she accused him of the attack?

George   Ah babes – I caught snippets of a heated convo from the balcony and filled large gaps myself.

Marcus   Nah, nah, nah, wait! Si and Andre had a fight?

George   Well, I dunno! He definitely was having a rant by the time I came down but whether it was at her I don't know. I asked him and he just shrugged it off.

Marcus   Andre? Fuck! You know what . . . that's why his mom kicked him out! I'm so stupid! I knew something didn't seem right but I just put it to the back of my head! That fucking prick!

George   Oi! Now we don't know that! God you're as bad as those boys out there!

Marcus   No! I do know. It makes sense!

George   Alright Sherlock! Quite a big accusation to throw at a sixteen-year-old boy that had the decency to stay with me this evening.

Marcus   I need to speak to him.

George   Well I'll be needing a strong word with your girlfriend.

Marcus   I dunno what's going on with her . . . we just had a bit of a fight . . .

George   Oh. Anything serious?

Marcus   No! Yeah, maybe.

George   Do we need wine? 'Cause I've been called a rapist and a 'paki lover' whilst attempts were made at my life.

Marcus   What?!

George   Shouted up from the street. I'm guessing it was meant for you.

Marcus   Ah hun, I'm so . . .

George   Don't you dare say you're sorry again!

Marcus   Right!

George   Pussy!

Marcus   Yep!

George   Wine!

Marcus   Lets go for it! I've already had a spliff downstairs.

George   And you're having a go at Soriya about cigarettes?

Marcus   I know! It was stress relief! Our secret?

George   Well I have more . . .

Marcus   I'll build, you get some glasses. Whoa! You necked this yourself already?

George   What part of being called a rapist did you not understand?

Marcus   Then you were clearly feeling guilty. (*Shakes the near empty bottle.*)

George   Of raping a girl? Busted!

Marcus *and* **George** *laugh.*

George   I shouldn't laugh. It may actually turn that way soon, anyway.

Marcus   What way?

George   Going for girls.

Marcus   Shut up! A gorgeous girl like you! What happened to the banker?

George   The white guy? Not really my type.

Marcus   And what is your type?

George   Well I've had the biggest crush on Si's brother since I was like thirteen but it didn't really work out, to Si's delight!

Marcus   Really?

George   I know! She's such a hater right?

Marcus   And now he's married.

George   Exactly! She could have ruined my life! If I'm still single when I hit thirty, I'll officially disown her! And put a curse on yours and hers relationship!

Marcus   We're into witchery now?

George   Oh yeah punk! And you two will be the first to get it!

Marcus   That's providing we're still together!

George   Stop being so wet! You guys have one little fight —

Marcus   Little?

George   You'll be fine. Do you feel to divulge?

Marcus   Why not? Soriya has now decided to marry a Pakistani.

George   What? Shut up! She doesn't even fancy Asian men.

Marcus   Well, apparently fancying someone is 'too short-term'.

George   What are you on about? Who has she met?

Marcus   Oh there's no one in particular. She's thinking of an arrangement.

George   Oh, hun. She's drunk and angry or something! You know how much stick she gave Ibi when he said he was gonna marry Umra?

Marcus   Well, that's what she's talking —

George   You have nothing to worry about. I know Soriya. She will never do that! Have you met Umra?

Marcus   No. She wasn't there when we had dinner —

George   Huh!

Marcus   I didn't want to question it . . .

George   You need to see her. Stunning girl. Young. They're first cousins, you know. No judgement, but seriously, she looks just like Soriya. Is that not wrong?

Marcus   I don't know . . .

George   Babes? Come on! It's like he's fucking his sister! It's wrong!

Marcus   Whoa! George man!

George   Someone has to say it. They think it's such a precious thing! It's not! And when I find someone and fall in love and live happily ever after, then Ibi will see what a mistake he made!

Marcus   Well good luck to you.

George   I hope so. I'm not looking for anything unrealistic. Just a nice guy.

Marcus   Nice? Hmmm . . .

George   Seriously! I hate guys that drive flash cars and am completely uninterested in pretentious jobs —

Marcus   Pretentious?

George   Jobs that they don't teach you in French . . .

Marcus   What?!

George   You know. 'My father is, my mom does . . .' Teachers, doctors, carpenters! Now they're normal jobs. Being the CEO of a blah blah blah that specialises in who gives a fuck . . .! Not interested!

Marcus   Ha! Fair point. What exactly do you think I do?

George   You're a business man.

Marcus   Ha! That makes me sound like a pimp! Or even worse a used-car salesman.

George   And what's so wrong with that?

Marcus   I think I'd rather be a pimp.

George   Yeah. Good point!

Marcus   Well, the football player? Si mentioned something about a premiership football player.

George   I don't know about premiership! He played for like the Gunners . . . team . . . or something. I wasn't really listening.

Marcus   Right . . . and . . . ? Anything there?

George   He was cute. Good arse.

Marcus   Of course!

George   Just . . . I think. I want someone I have something in common with.

Marcus   Have you been speaking to Soriya?

George   What? Oh. Babes, common interests don't begin with matching skin tone! I have more chance of ending up with a black guy than a white guy if we're gonna base it on common interests!

Marcus   And what do you have in common with them?

George *stands.*

George   Babes! I'm from 'the junc'! Holiday in Tobago at least twice annually. LOVE curry goat and roti. Drive an X5 with a bigger engine size than yours, listen to grime, wear 'bling', from Links of London of course, and so am technically more street than you or any 'brear' from off that fucking Westbridge estate!

Marcus *laughs while* **George** *takes a bow.*

Marcus   You're too good for everyone round here! Black, white, street —

George   Posh?

Marcus   Yeah!

George   Thanks. Like I said. I know what I want. It's not unattainable and I have no intention of settling until I get it spot on.

Silence. **George** *leans towards* **Marcus**.

Marcus   What are you doing?

George   I don't know.

Marcus   Look, no. Sorry if I misled you but . . . no.

George   No, I'm sorry. Everything about this, us chilling here, is just reminding me of someone and it's confusing me.

Marcus   OK. We cool?

George   Our secret?

Marcus nods. *Lights fade to the sound of sirens and more havoc.*

Scene Nine

Saghir's *house. The next morning. We hear a radio news bulletin reporting on last night's riots.*

Ibi   Dad! Come on! Hurry up, eh? I promised chacha-ji we'd be two in the shop from open!

Saghir (*o/s*)   They are not going to let us trade today! I promise you! There will be more police warnings after last night, there's no point.

Ibi   Dad! Just hurry, yeah!

Saghir   I can't find my phone! Where have you put it?

Ibi   Try calling it!

Saghir   I can't hear it!

Ibi   Dad come on!

George enters.

George   Hey.

Ibi   Hey! Two mornings in a row?

George   Yeah. I've just driven past the shop.

Ibi   Yeah?

George   Have you not been there yet?

Ibi   No, on our way now, why?

George   Look, it's all fixable. I took a couple of pictures. It didn't look like they'd managed to get inside so . . .

George *hands* **Ibi** *her phone.*

Ibi   Shit!

George   You OK?

Ibi   Yeah. Everything is covered but . . . looks like we might just be out of action for a bit I guess.

George   Well they'll be sorry when they have to go all the way to the high street for a bottle of milk.

Ibi   Maybe.

George   It's not just you guys. The entire street looks like . . . well . . . I'm sure you can gather.

Ibi   Bet the French deli looks fine.

George   It'll be OK.

Ibi   Yeah. Shit! Si's gone home if you're looking for her.

George   I actually came to see you.

Ibi   Oh, right. Look George, now's not the best time . . .

George   Yeah. Of course . . . Well, no, I just came to share some good news.

Ibi   Yeah?

George   Just ended up emailing over a couple of pictures to that agency yesterday lunchtime and they've got me my first job!

Ibi   That quick?

George   I didn't even need to audition. They cast me straight from the photos!

Ibi   Cool. What's it for?

George   You are now looking at the new face of Pizza Hut.

Ibi   Congratulations?

George   I tried to get out of it.

Ibi   Why?

George   I told the agent it wasn't realistic for someone with my skin quality and physique to eat at the hut.

Ibi   And what did they say to that?

George   The commercial's worth eight grand and if I turn it down and lose their commission they'll have to strike me from their books.

Ibi   Strict. What did you say to that?

George   See you Monday.

Ibi *laughs*.

George   Yeah . . .

Ibi   Look. I'm so sorry for the way I spoke to you yesterday. I have the utmost respect for you and I don't know . . . I guess I was just angry and scared . . .

George   Scared?

Ibi   Scared I'd not made the right decision.

George   Ibi I want to tell you something —

Ibi   No. Let me finish. Since the wedding I'd felt so distant to Umra. It's not what I imagined being married to be like and it's . . . an adjustment.

George   Of course . . .

Ibi   I mean I have tried so hard to please her, impress her even and the response was . . . nothing.

George   Ibi . . .

Ibi So all those insecurities that were bugging me I just let them rip on you.

George If you can sense something's not right . . .

Ibi But then, please don't say anything, but seeing how quickly Marcus and Si almost crumbled over the smallest thing? I mean come on, some old lady made a comment and their world's collapsed. That could never happen to us and that gives me confidence, strength even. Does that sound cocky?

George But you can't really compare —

Ibi I mean there's still a slight language barrier but my Punjabi's getting much better and her English is so much stronger and I think that's the reason for not feeling as close as we should.

George Ibi, I worry that . . .

Ibi And I love her George! I really do!

George You do?

Ibi I mean I didn't even think it would be possible to feel like this about her so . . . so soon I guess. But I've never felt like this about anyone.

George Anyone . . .?

Ibi Ah! George! That came out wrong. This is just different, I guess, and feels so right. You understand yeah?

George Yes.

Ibi Sorry. What were you trying to say?

Saghir *enters.*

George Oh erm . . . I can't even remember.

Saghir I give up! It's lost! Georgina?!

George Hello *Abba* !

Saghir   Hello darling! You OK?! You hungry? You want tea?

George   Oh I'm OK thank you. Trying this new diet thing.

Saghir   Diet! There's nothing to you! This is why you are single! Men like meat!

George   Love you too, *Abba*!

Saghir (*indicating the food tray*)   Here!

George   Thank you.

Ibi   Look Dad. George just saw the shop.

Saghir   They've trashed it?!

Ibi   Here.

Ibi *passes* **Saghir** *the phone.*

Ibi   Dad. Don't worry. We'll be covered.

Saghir   What is that? (*Reads.*) 'Go Home Pak . . .' Ah!

Ibi   Ah Dad. It's just kids.

Saghir   Maybe. It's just sad that despite how long I've lived here. Despite having two British children. Despite learning their British fucking language – I will never be that.

Ibi   What? British? Who cares?

Saghir   I care. This is my home and I'm not going anywhere!

Ibi   No one expects you to.

Saghir   Someone does!

Ibi   That's probably a couple of kids that couldn't give a toss either way – they just enjoyed the chance to do a little vandalism. Excitement!

Saghir   I need my phone!

Ibi   Here. Use mine.

Ibi *passes* **Saghir** *his mobile.*

Saghir   Come, we have to go down there!

Saghir *exits.*

Ibi   We've got to . . .

George   Yeah! Of course.

Ibi   Are you gonna stay?

George   No, no. I'm just gonna check my face but I'll let myself out.

Ibi   OK, see you George.

George   Bye.

Ibi *exits. Lights.*

Scene Ten

Outside the shop on the Westbridge. **Saghir** *on his mobile phone.*

Saghir   Yes. I understand. So, what happens now? Well I'm outside the shop. Do I have to stay here?

But there's no way to secure it?

Oh, OK. And what time will that be?

But we don't need to be here?

I understand. Thank you.

Ibi *enters.*

Ibi   That's all we're gonna get in the car.

Saghir   Come, let's just go home.

Ibi *turns and exits in the direction he came.* **Audrey** *enters from the opposite side. She stops after noticing* **Saghir** *first and then the shop. She offers a half smile.* **Saghir** *returns it with a head nod.* **Audrey** *crosses in front of him in silence, continuing her journey.* **Saghir** *watches her pass.* **Audrey** *exits.* **Saghir** *takes one last look at his shop and then exits.*

Scene Eleven

Private garage on the Westbridge estate. As before.

Andre   Tst! Oi!

Sara   Hey mister!

Andre   Sorry I'm late!

Sara   You will be!

Andre   Yeah yeah! What happened to your — (face).

She flinches and looks away

Andre   Him?

Beat.

Andre   I wish you'd tell someone!

Sara   Like who? The police?

Andre   What about your sister?

Sara   She agrees with Dad.

Andre   That's messed up! I wish . . . I wish —

Sara   'Low it! They'll get over it! Just sometimes you gotta ride things out.

Andre   Why don't you come stay with me for a bit at the hostel?

Sara   Andre the hero!

Andre   Why not? I could sneak you in easy!

Sara   You're not serious? That would give them ammunition to kill me!

Andre   They wouldn't know where you were! It'd teach 'em a lesson.

Sara   Nah! I've got no reason to act guilty. I work hard at school. Help out at home. They wouldn't have a problem with me having a boyfriend, except that it's you. That makes them wrong not me.

Andre   And what? They're just gonna keep punching you in the face until you stop?

Sara   They're pissed. They'll calm down.

Andre   They've tried to call me a fucking rapist.

Sara   We got caught dude. By Dad's friend. What else could he say? That was mortifying! I would never have lived that down.

Andre   Sounds like you're glad he did that.

Sara   Well in a way I am. I'm a young girl. My reputation would have been ruined . . .

Andre   What reputation? You're telling me you're gonna be with me the rest of your life so only what I think of you matters.

Sara   I know. And I love you, but let's be realistic. I'd love to be with you forever but if it don't work . . .

Andre   Why wouldn't it work?

Sara   Just saying innit, if it don't work, I'm screwed. I'm the one with the damaged rep. Not you. No one would want to touch me.

Andre   I want to touch you.

Sara   I want you to touch me.

Andre   Where? There?

Sara   Maybe . . .

Andre *kisses her.*

Andre   There?

Andre *and* **Sara** *kiss again. It quickly turns into more.* **Marcus** *enters talking into his mobile.*

Marcus   I'll be at my mom's. Please, Si, just call me back.

Marcus *instantly notices* **Andre** *and* **Sara**.

Marcus   Ah, are you serious?

Andre   You don't know about knocking?

Marcus   For who?

Andre   This ain't your space fam! Ain't you got a yard to be chilling in?

Marcus   Same way you have a hostel to be getting back to innit? Who's she?

Andre   It's my bredrin from school.

Marcus   Oh you two are *friends*?

Sara   Yes.

Marcus   You live on Westbridge too?

Sara   No, erm . . .

Andre   She lives across the way.

Marcus   And yet you're such good friends.

Andre   No —

Marcus   Course not 'cause you don't even really go school do you?

Andre   Differently, we were trying to have a private convo so if you don't mind . . .

Marcus   Convo? I think that's where it's all going wrong for you Andre. If that's how you insist on talking to girls.

Andre   Look. What do you want?

Marcus   Who you stepping to, you fucking prick?!

Andre   Dickhead!

Marcus   What did you just say?!

Marcus *drags up* **Andre** *viciously and acts as though he's going to hit him.* **Andre** *is very shocked by this reaction.*

Andre   Nothing. I didn't say nothing.

Marcus *lets him go.*

Marcus   I can't believe I just caught little Andre having sex! I mean don't get me wrong, I was definitely boning girls by the time I was your age but still it's odd to see. I proper think of you as a rugrat!

Andre   Yeah well I'm not!

Marcus   Having sex ay? In the estate where that girl got raped. You got a proper little thing for Indian girls don't you?

Andre   What are you on about? I'm sixteen! I've a thing for all girls!

Marcus   And yet you only seem to get caught fucking the Asian ones.

Andre   Ones? The only 'one' I've been fucking is her? That's my wife you prick!

Marcus   Well that's a lie ain't it? I mean you fucked some next girl last week. (*Whispers.*) Against her will. (*Turning to* **Sara**.) Did you know about that? The girl that got attacked? It was your boyfriend that 'attacked' her.

Andre   Oh my days! SHUT UP! What girl? What fucking girl? Will people just drop it! If you can't name her or point her out how can you be so protective of her!

Marcus (*grabs him again*)   'Cause she was a youte. Family friends with Si that you put your grubby hands on! And I can't even get into the dramz that's causing me.

Andre   I didn't touch no one! There was no one to touch!

Marcus   You fucking perverted liar! What?

Marcus *lays into* **Andre**, *slapping him repeatedly in the face. It's more to humiliate than to injure.*

Sara   Oi! Stop it! Stop it!

Marcus   What part of your man's a rapist did you not hear?

Through struggle **Andre** *falls to the floor.*

You make me sick! After everything your mom's done for you.

Marcus *kicks him out of anger. Throughout the rest of his rant he continuously kicks* **Andre**.

Marcus   And I swear to god you ever try talk to Soriya in a way again! Nah, you ever try to talk to her! I'll fucking kill you! Think you're a badman? Huh? Huh?!

Sara   Help! Help! Please! Somebody help us!

Marcus *then steps back, having shocked himself.*

Sara   Andre! Andre! I'm so sorry! Please be OK. I didn't know. I swear. I had no idea people knew it was you. I had know idea people knew my name! Please, please be OK! Andre! Please! I love you! I want to be with you. If you get through this I promise I will tell everyone the truth about us! I don't care anymore. I just want to be with you. Andre. Andre!

Marcus *hears* **Sara**'s *mumblings and is confused.*

Soriya (*from off*)   Marcus!

Soriya *enters.*

Soriya   Marcus!

On hearing **Soriya**'s *voice* **Sara** *panics, backs away and exits.*

Marcus   Si!

Soriya (*seeing* **Andre**)   What's going on?

Andre *begins to stand, visibly hurt.*

Marcus   Well here you are. The perfect excuse to leave me. Take it!

Soriya   Is that what you think I'm doing? Looking for excuses? Andre? Are you OK?!

Andre   Don't touch me! What you even doing here?

Soriya   I just saw Marcus's car . . . are you OK?

Andre   Why act like you care?

Andre *stands and touches his face for damage. His nose is bleeding.*

Soriya   You're hurt.

Andre   I'm fine. And I'll be fine.

Soriya   Marcus!

Marcus   What?

Soriya   Don't talk to me like that.

Marcus   Like what? What?! This is just how I talk, ennit?!

Soriya   Stop it!

Andre   Where's Sara?

Marcus   You blind? She dipped! Soon as she heard Si. Loyal!

Soriya   What?

Andre   What did you say to her?

Soriya   How do you know Sara, Andre?

Marcus   I didn't say anything.

Soriya   Andre?

Andre   If you scared her?

Marcus   How? She ducked off. She don't care about you.

Andre   Nah, she's just probably scared. And I'm not surprised. Your girl's a snake!

Soriya   Answer my question!

Andre   I'm sorry, but really who are you to me? Ain't it obvious?

Marcus   Watch it.

Soriya   Isn't what obvious?

Marcus   Si just leave it

Andre   Yeah, Si, leave it!

Marcus   I ain't warning you again!

Soriya   Will someone explain?

Andre   She's my girl! Sara's my girl.

Soriya   But when she was raped . . .

Andre   Are you really that dumb? No one was raped! She was with me and her dad's friend didn't like it!

Soriya   They said you raped her.

Andre   Bit more entertaining, innit?

Andre *sits down to make a phone call. No one answers. He redials.*

Soriya (*to* **Marcus**)   Did you know, before?

Marcus   Why the fuck would I know?

Soriya   What is with you?

Marcus   Are you serious? You wanna know what's with me?

Soriya   We'll talk when we get home, OK?

Marcus   Why? You might as well just say what you're saying, here! Who cares anymore? Fucking talk.

Soriya   Stop swearing at me!

Marcus   Talk! Soriya! You're telling me you don't want to be with me. I'm too different! Too mixed up for you! So what am I risking? Huh? TALK!

Soriya   I have doubts! I'm sorry.

Marcus   Well as long as you're sorry . . .

Soriya   I can't believe you hit him.

Marcus   Really?! I'm a black man from Westbridge. Is that not just what we do?!

Andre   You ain't black fam.

Marcus   You what?

Andre   You heard. And you ain't from round here neither. Not really. Not the Westbridge. We don't churn out dickheads like you.

Marcus   Well I'm sorry to disappoint.

Andre   Mock all you want. But you're the one arguing on street with gal and for what? Nothing's really wrong. Nothing tragic has happened. Has it? You're not homeless, say, with a mom who don't trust you. You've not got the entire neighbourhood where you live putting a question mark above your head. And on top of all that. The thing that would have made it all worthwhile . . .

Andre *breaks.*

Marcus   Andre . . .

Andre   What?! I'm fine.

Marcus   Go home.

Andre   Is that a joke?

Marcus   You just gonna stay here?

Andre   She might come back.

Marcus   You're gonna wait for her?

Andre   Well I can hardly go to hers, can I?

Marcus   I don't get it! Is she worth all this?

Andre   I've got no choice. I love her.

Marcus   Andre. It don't have to be this hard. I love Si, but —

Andre   Nah soz fam. You don't. And she don't love you. You both just enjoy fucking each other 'cause it's exciting. You're not really supposed to be together, so it's dangerous. But at the end of the day, that's all it is – a good bang! That's why you don't get it. You know what, 'low it. I'll wait outside.

Andre *has been calling someone throughout. They're not answering. He exits.*

Soriya   He didn't do anything.

Marcus   As you said, that's not even the issue anymore.

The End.

Printed in the USA
CPSIA information can be obtained
at www.ICGtesting.com
LVHW020844171024
794056LV00002B/385